CRUSHING YOUTUBE

HOW TO MAKE MONEY ON YOUTUBE AND GROW A CHANNEL FAST

FROM ZERO TO 75,000 SUBSCRIBERS IN 18 MONTHS

THE POWER OF YOUTUBE

How is a 7-year old making over $22 million a year? How is a slacker gamer reaching an average of 10 million people every time he uploads a video?

How have I been able to create a monthly income of $7,000 in less than 18 months?

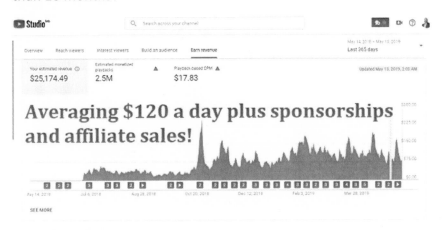

That's the power of YouTube!

Now you've probably heard all the complaining about YouTube changing its policies, how difficult it is to make money on the site. You've probably even heard more than a few people say, "YouTube is Dead!"

Don't believe it for a second.

I've been able to grow a channel from just 22 subscribers to over 75,000 since December 2017 and sta`rted mentoring new channels in 2019. In that time, I've seen new subscribers reach tens of thousands of subscribers and make thousands a month. All within a year of starting their channel.

Now I'm not saying you'll become the next Ryan Kaji, the seven-year old star of Ryan's Toy Review, making over $20 million a year. You probably won't become the next PewDiePie, the ex-gamer turned influencer with 95 million subscribers.

You might not become a YouTube sensation but you can create a six-figure income and an online asset that reaches millions of people every year.

But you need to know the business of YouTube! You need a strategy!

More than 99.6% of the 26 million-plus channels on YouTube have less than 100,000 subscribers and nine-in-ten have less than the 1,000 subscriber requirement to join the partner program and make money off their videos.

More than 300 hours of video is uploaded to YouTube every minute. Millions of channels compete for the two billion monthly users. It's not impossible for a new channel to compete but you'll need a strategy and you need to know how the platform works.

You could spend the next two years watching how-to videos on YouTube. That's the average time it takes most creators to get to 1,000 subscribers. You could watch the all the YouTube gurus and hope you find everything to make your strategy work.

Or you can spend a couple of weeks to get the tools you need to grow your channel.

That's how long it will take to get through this book. Just a couple of weeks to read through the book, work through the examples and apply it to your YouTube channel. When you're done, you'll have everything you need to grow your channel and you WILL be successful!

What you'll learn:

- The secrets to setting up your channel that will drive views and subscribers (page 33)
- How to get video ideas and hack the most popular videos in your topic for instant success (page 49)
- Five steps to building a brand on YouTube that creates a community that will support you on every video (page 69)

- The easy way to record videos, even if you don't like to be on camera (page 85)
- The growth hack even YouTube stars aren't using that will take your channel to the next level (page 123)
- Five income streams you MUST be using to make money on YouTube and every step to get started (page 135)

Whether you want to make thousands a month through a channel or just create a platform that takes your message to millions of people, this book will give you the strategy to accomplish it. You will never find a more comprehensive guide to starting and growing a YouTube channel!

What Other YouTube Creators are Saying about Crushing YouTube,

"Crushing YouTube should be required reading for anyone wanting to start, or grow, a YouTube channel. If you apply the tips Joseph shares in this book, your message WILL reach more people." *Devin Carroll*

Joseph is at the forefront of YouTube channel growth, experimenting, improving, and strategizing his way to YouTube success. This book provides a clear roadmap from start to finish if you want to grow a vibrant YouTube channel. *Colin Jones, Blackjack Apprenticeship*

"I'm so grateful to have followed Joseph's advice on my YouTube channel and content optimization. As a result, my channel grew much faster than expected and I was able to attract a sponsor for my channel within my first two months! Take action on everything you read. It really does work." *Josh Elledge, UpMyInfluence*

"Watching Joseph's channel grow has been an inspiration to me, and the advice I've received from him has put my channel on the path of progress again. It's clear that he is a great teacher, and an even better YouTuber, Thank you!" *David Pere, From Military to Millionaire*

Joseph Hogue, CFA

Born and raised in Iowa, Joseph Hogue graduated from Iowa State University after serving in the Marine Corps. He worked in corporate finance and real estate before starting a career in investment analysis. He has appeared on Bloomberg and CNBC and led a team of equity analysts for a venture capital research firm. He holds a master's degree in business and the Chartered Financial Analyst (CFA) designation.

Joseph left the corporate world in 2014 to build his online businesses, first through creating websites and later through YouTube. Booking just $792.41 in 2015 income, he's grown his online assets to an income of $122,400 for the twelve-months to July 2019. He's published 10 books and has grown the YouTube channel, Let's Talk Money, to over 75,000 subscribers in just 18 months.

TABLE OF CONTENTS

I WANT TO BE A PART OF YOUR JOURNEY…

Through writing this book, I wanted a closer connection with would-be YouTube creators. There were also parts where I wanted to add more detail, not through text but through an actual live walk-throughs of the process. The book gives you everything you need to grow a channel that reaches millions but I wanted to offer something more.

The answer, a companion video course!

Through informal videos, I could do more than I dreamed possible through just text alone. I could show you exactly what I'm doing on my computer while researching the video ideas that go viral. I could show you my video setup and the exact social strategy that brings me thousands of views, all step-by-step.

This is the video guide you need to make sure you get every detail, follow every step and grow your YouTube channel fast to make as much money as possible!

In the video course, you'll get:
- Videos for each chapter with on-screen explanations and additional content.
- Access to a private Facebook group where we help each other and keep you updated on what's working!
- An 8-week email series to keep you on schedule and help guide you through the most important points.
- Lifetime access to the course, Q&A and resources to grow your channel
- Bonus!! A free channel review to make sure you get started right!

I average $3,500 a month on YouTube ads alone along with more than $3,000 on sponsorships and affiliate marketing. This course WILL pay for itself inside of six months!

Watch this Free Preview Video and Get a Special 35% Discount
Or visit https://myworkfromhomemoney.com/YTCommunity

THE ONLY ONLINE INCOME SOURCE THAT ISN'T DYING!

I remember my first financial bloggers conference in 2015. I was so excited to be getting into the world of blogging and start making the tens of thousands of dollars I saw other bloggers reporting.

On the first day, the keynote speaker shook my world. He said, "Blogging is Dead!"

The message wasn't exactly that you couldn't make money blogging. It was that you had to do more than just make money on advertising from your blog, the default income source to that point. Now sponsorships and affiliate marketing were the big money-maker.

So I did that. I concentrated on boosting my sponsorship and affiliate game to make money.

The very next year, the same financial bloggers conference... somebody said, "Affiliate marketing and sponsored posts are dead!"

WTF! It seems people had gotten tired of affiliates and sponsored posts and just weren't clicking anymore. Now you had to be creating courses to make any money.

You can guess what happened the next year...yep, "Courses are dead!"

Through this entire time, through the emergence and death of so many income ideas, there is one online source that has only gotten stronger.

YouTube.

YouTube creators continue to grow massive channels, continue to grow their income and continue to grow their reach.

I got fed up with all the other 'dead' income sources and finally got serious about my own YouTube channel in December 2017.

It was Christmas Day, I had 22 subscribers and finally made the commitment to grow the channel as an asset.

Just 18 months later, as I type the last words in this guide, I've grown the channel to over 75,000 subscribers. I average over $3,500 a month in ads on the platform and more than $3,000 each month in product sales and sponsorships.

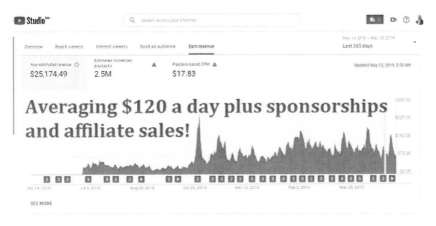

YouTube is most definitely not "dead"!

In fact, there is a good argument that YouTube won't fade out like so many of the other online income strategies. The differences between the video platform and other online media creates natural barriers to entry that protect those successful few.

- Most people don't feel comfortable on camera and are 'afraid' to put themselves out there.

- Those that do make the leap to creating a channel find they don't have the time for the pre-production, filming, editing and marketing necessary to be successful.

- Most people don't know how to monetize a distribution platform like YouTube, settling to just make money off ads (which are at best only half the potential income).

- Despite my success, and the strategy in this book that got me there, it is very difficult to grow a channel from scratch to the point of making thousands a month.

These four factors help keep YouTube from getting overwhelmed by new channels and new competition. I write that knowing full well the statistic that 300+ minutes of video are uploaded to the platform every minute. Despite the 26 million-plus channels on YouTube, it will always be a money-making platform for those with the strategy to be successful.

I feel like I'm 'preaching to the choir' on this. In reading this book, you've obviously already made the commitment to be successful on YouTube. How much further convincing do you really need?

No, I'm not saying this to convince you but to keep you motivated. There will be times when you question your commitment. You will occasionally hear from some frustrated creator that YouTube is "dead".

Don't believe it for a second. Read through the book. Watch the accompanying videos and know that your hard work WILL be rewarded. Know that factors unique to creating a video channel will mean a solid and growing income for years to come. Know that the strategy laid out in this book WILL get you there!

Let's get to it!

HOW TO PICK A TOPIC ON YOUTUBE

Picking a topic on YouTube is important but more important is how your channel will be different

The average person sees more than 5,000 commercials a day from traditional TV spots to banner ads and links. There are millions of blogs online and 300 hours of video are uploaded to YouTube EVERY SINGLE MINUTE!

How does anyone ever stand out in this crowd?

The answer is to not be all things to all people. Instead of trying to reach the 30 million daily visitors on YouTube, you're going to be a must-watch channel for a small fraction of that audience.

And you do that by picking a topic, or in marketing terms, 'a niche'.

What is a Niche?

A niche is just a technical term for a very specific group, the primary group attracted to what you talk about.

Now your videos might attract a wide range of casual viewers. Lots of people are interested in making money or investing. You're certainly not going to exclude them.

By defining your niche, you're narrowing what you plan on talking about on the channel. You're going to say, "I'm not going to be all things to all people but I am an expert in this!" Defining your niche will help you with video ideas, ranking higher and building a more loyal community.

We'll talk about narrowing your niche but generally you start with a broad topic, study the channels in the topic and then narrow your focus to a sub-topic or group within that so you can compete more easily.

An example of a niche might be within personal finance, you decide to talk about making money online. I would suggest this is still a little too broad so maybe you narrow it further to just blogging or a particular income source. You might even narrow your focus to a demographic group like stay-at-home moms or college students.

How YouTube is Different from Google and other Social Media

For the bloggers and social media influencers, building a channel on YouTube will be a little different. You've still got the idea of an algorithm, say on Google or Facebook, that is determining how (and whether) to promote your content but YouTube does it in a way that makes your niche even more important.

YouTube serves your new videos to a section of your subscribers first, usually to the subscribers that have also watched videos similar to your new content. This is mostly done in the subscriber's home page and subscription feed.

Your success with that initial group, the number that clicks on the video, determines how far and wide YouTube will promote it further. If many of your subscribers click on the video, YouTube will send it out to more subscribers and to some non-subscribers that have watched similar content. If that group of non-subscribers also clicks to watch the video, the platform will expand the reach even further.

The platform keeps doing this, continuously using data from who is clicking and how much of the video they watch, to determine how much further to expand your video's reach.

So what does this mean to your niche and why is it important?

Think about it from the perspective of someone with no definable niche, a person that posts videos with no clear content strategy. People that subscribe to their channel may do so because they like the creator's personality but they aren't likely to be interested in a lot of the content.

That means there might not be many of your subscribers from that initial test group that will be interested in the new video. They won't click through and it will be a negative signal to YouTube...even the subscribers aren't interested so why push it out to more people?

That's going to make it difficult to grow a channel in the first place if your videos aren't being promoted much by YouTube.

Now think of it in terms of someone that posts videos only on a very specific niche. It's much more likely that all their subscribers are going to be interested in this new video because it is similar to the videos that attracted them to the channel. More of those subscribers are going to click on the new video, sending YouTube a positive signal to send the video out further.

There's another aspect to this that's also important for established channels, switching topics. If you've built a following or even just recently released a series of videos on a specific topic, switching to another topic can be painful in terms of views.

There are two problems here. If you've built a following in one particular niche, then that's what your subscribers are interested in seeing. They might not necessarily be interested in something else, even if it's related to your niche. Again, that lack of interest from subscribers will limit your video's reach.

The other problem, and this is one I see all the time, is that a big part of that initial group of subscribers YouTube tests on your new video are the ones that have recently joined your community. YouTube wants to see if they are going to be regular consumers of your content or if they were only interested in that one video.

Let's look at an example and the problem will become clear. I talk about investing and making money on the channel, both topics have to do with money but the audience wouldn't necessarily be the same.

If I do a series of six investing videos over two weeks, many of my new subscribers are going to be those interested in investing. If I then switch over to doing a week or two of videos about making money, those new subscribers are likely in that initial test group to see the video in their feed…and may not be interested in watching.

This doesn't mean you can't be successful with videos in different (but related) topics. It's part of understanding the YouTube algorithm, how it determines which videos to promote and how to work within that system.

How to Pick Your Niche

So if your topic on YouTube is so important, how do you pick a topic?

Passion, Expertise and Money!

There's a lot of advice on picking a topic whether you're starting a YouTube channel, a blog or even a business. It can all be boiled down to those three words.

What do you enjoy talking about, what's your passion? You're going to be doing a lot of research, writing and talking about this topic. It might be a while before you make any real money for that paycheck motivation. You better enjoy talking about it. Besides that, people will sense your passion for the material and that enthusiasm will be contagious.

That means listing out your hobbies, interests and that bucket list of things you always wanted to do.

What do you have deep experience doing? This is something you can build but it always helps if you're not starting from scratch. Often this is what you do for a living or at least an idea within that industry.

This should be secondary to your interests though. I've seen people start their blog as a journey in a completely new topic, taking readers on the journey as they learn. It's a great way to build a community and can work just as well as starting from expertise.

Finally is the money! What's the most profitable niche? This is third to the other two considerations and really only as a deciding point among different ideas. For example, if you have a passion and experience in both Self-Publishing and Underwater Horseback Riding...I'd say go with Self-Publishing as a topic.

An easy way to find how 'monetizable' a topic can be is to look in your Google Adsense account. You can search for keywords related to the topic and Google will tell you the average cost per click for ads. Topics and keywords with a higher cost will mean YouTube channels related to those topics serving ads will make more money.

Narrowing your Topic into a Niche

Once you've got an idea of a broader topic, something in which you're interested and have some experience, it's time to start narrowing it into a niche.

Developing a niche is all about speaking specifically to a smaller group of people. You can narrow your topic and/or narrow your audience.

For example, instead of talking broadly about investing, you might narrow your content to dividend investing or real estate investing. Both of these ideas still interest tens of millions of people but are not as broad as the general topic. Many investors might ONLY be interested in dividends or real estate so you'll be able to reach that group much more effectively.

You can also narrow your niche by personal traits; targeting a generational group, gender or even people in a specific region. These have less to do with the topic and more to do with the group that relates best to your personality.

This isn't about being exclusionary or limiting yourself to a very narrow group of people. Your videos may still appeal to a broad range of viewers. Being specific in your niche is about speaking to the heart of that narrow group.

Because of how the YouTube algorithm works, a community of 1,000 subscribers that is very engaged and clicks on every video will beat a much larger channel of casual-subscribers for ranking.

By narrowing your niche, you're building that every-video loyalty with enough subscribers that gives each new video a jumpstart so YouTube will promote it out to an ever-larger audience.

Finding Your Different-ness

There's one more important idea that's not necessarily related to selecting your niche but will help you be successful.

This is the idea of being different and it goes a long way to building a brand on YouTube.

There were more than 26 million channels on YouTube as of 2018. In all that competition, you can have some of the most informative content in your niche...and still have trouble building your community.

Best-selling author Sally Hogshead is credited with a quote that is pure genius saying, "Different is better than better."

How is your channel different from the thousands, even millions in your niche? How is anyone going to remember your channel after watching ten or twenty videos in a day?

For example, I could just put on a t-shirt for my YouTube videos. It seems to be the de facto uniform for most channels and the ultimate in comfort. Instead, not only am I sending a message by wearing a shirt and bowtie, it's also quite different from what people are used to seeing.

Your 'different-ness' can come in many forms from what you wear, your speaking style, graphics, sound effects and even the background in your videos.

Writing this section, I couldn't help but think about some of the great stand-up comedians of the 80s...and yes I know I'm old. They might not have been any funnier than others but everyone remembers Steven Wright for his unique 'depressed, lethargic' persona and Sam Kinison for his screaming act. These guys were nothing if not different and people will always remember their act.

We'll talk more about the idea of being different in building your brand but think about how you can be different in content, visual cues and your message.

Picking your YouTube topic and niche is where it all starts and is more important that most creators know. This will set the stage for where your videos compete for rank and how you build a community of subscribers. Spend some time to really think about where you want to make your mark and how you can be different.

Action Steps:
- Write out a list of things you enjoy doing, hobbies and all the things on your bucket list.
- Start with a topic in mind and drill down at least one or two levels. For example, if you want to talk about personal finance then you might pick the sub-topic of budgeting and then even more narrowly-focused on saving money.
- Create a story around the person that would most enjoy your videos. Who are they, what do they do on a daily basis? This initial picture of your target audience is going to help

you in not only building your niche but also branding later on.

- Find five channels that serve your niche and watch some of their videos. How can you be different either in content, visually or in branding?

7 YOUTUBE CHANNEL GOALS YOU CAN CONTROL

Making the right YouTube channel goals will mean the difference between failure and success

YouTube can be frustrating...like digging the Grand Canyon with a teaspoon frustrating!

You spend hours learning how to develop a channel. You spend hours planning your content and strategy, hours more shooting and editing videos, and yet it can seem like your subscriber count barely ticks higher.

Setting goals is one of the core tenants in Steven Covey's almost sacred book on business, "The 7 Habits of Highly Effective People," and it's no less important when planning your future as a video star.

Setting the right goals can push you to achieve something marvelous. The right goals will motivate you before and after you've achieved them.

The wrong goals will do exactly the opposite though. Setting bad goals will demoralize you, make you feel like a loser and will weigh you down.

The problem is, starting out on YouTube, I guarantee the very first goal you made...is the wrong goal.

I'm going to share my experience with this bad goal that destroys most YouTube channels as well as seven YouTube goals you should be making instead.

My YouTube Goals

First, I want to share the most common mistake made when people start a YouTube channel. I made it. Most would-be YouTube stars make it and it keeps them from realizing the success that should be theirs.

Being a type-A personality, I've always felt a comfort in making goals and planning. Having everything organized and having those goals just feels like I'm driving to a destination rather than on some meandering Sunday drive.

So when I decided to develop my YouTube channel as a business asset in December 2017, I sat down to write out my goals for growth.

The first was to reach 1,000 subscribers by the end of 2018.

It would still be a couple months before YouTube changed its policy on monetization that required channels have over 1,000 subs to profit from ads. Even before this, I knew from research that channels beyond this point seemed to get more views and have some kind of additional momentum.

Reaching 1,000 subscribers told YouTube, you're here to win and the platform seemed to reward that commitment.

I had friends that were on YouTube for years and hadn't reached the mark yet. I had researched articles that pegged the average time to build 1,000 subs at somewhere around two years. Taking all this, I though 1,000 subs in a year would be a good stretch goal.

Then reality set in. I was creating videos, applying everything I had learned about developing a channel, but my subscriber count was just not increasing as quickly as I thought it should.

That frustration quickly turned to excitement when an older video started ranking for some strong keywords and really took off. My subscriber count jumped and I passed 1,000 subs in early March.

I wasn't about to sit on my success though so I made a new goal of 10,000 subs by the end of the year. It was here that I could unlock the Community Tab on the channel (this is now available to channels with over 1,000 subscribers).

The views kept coming in though, especially when another two videos started performing, and I hit that 10K goal in July.

While I was ecstatic that my channel was growing so quickly, there was also an uneasy worry creeping up in the back of my mind. I had beaten my goals but it felt like it was completely out of my control!

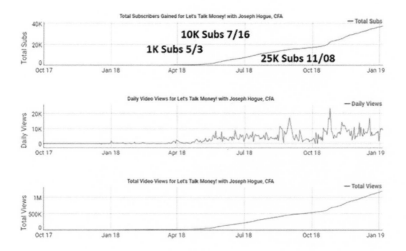

I hadn't really done much differently for the three runaway videos than I had done for dozens of others. I had switched to two videos a week and adopted a few ideas we'll talk about through the book, but there was seemingly nothing I was doing that was directly controlling the subscriber count.

This is the problem so many people have with creating subscriber or view count goals on YouTube.

There is nothing you can do to make a video go viral. There is nothing you can do to directly boost your subscriber count.

It's great if everything comes together and your subscriber count zooms past your goals, but what happens when it's the opposite problem? What happens when you create quality videos, have a solid marketing plan and do everything right…and your subscriber count barely budges?

Not meeting your goals, especially after so much hard work, can make you feel like a failure. It can leave you hopeless and feeling like none of your hard work matters.

It's a feeling faced by too many YouTubers, ones that would eventually be huge success stories, but who give up because of missing their subscriber goal.

I realized mid-year that subscriber goals were the wrong way to measure YouTube success. If I was going to work to a goal, it would have to be something I could control through working harder and smarter. Of course, I wanted to pick goals that would influence views and subscriber count, but I wasn't going to hang my success on something over which I had no control.

Creating YouTube Goals You Can Control

None of this means you shouldn't make goals for your YouTube channel. Goals motivate and drive us; they keep us from giving up and give us a sense of progress.

The key is to create goals around actions you can control. While you might not be able to control how many views a video gets or your subscriber count, you can create goals around actions that will directly influence the growth of your channel.

It's these goals that are going to drive the success of your channel.

I'll share the seven goals I make for my YouTube business but I don't want you to think these are the only ones out there. Making your own goals, just remember the rule to create goals around actions you can control and that will drive more views and subscribers.

Upload Consistency and Frequency – This is probably the most important goal you can make for your channel. Understand that YouTube wants to be a TV alternative for viewers. To do that, it needs creators that produce quality content consistently and on the same schedule.

There's two points here you need to remember, that consistency and frequency.

Frequency is the number of times per week you publish. Once a week used to be enough to grow a channel but twice a week is quickly becoming the benchmark. Understand that YouTube gives new videos preferential ranking for the first few days so uploading multiple times a week will make sure you always have a video getting that artificial boost.

I know it's tough juggling a full-time job and trying to grow your YouTube channel. If you're serious about making this a business, make a goal of uploading two videos a week. Eventually, you'll want to increase that to three days a week and someday to five days for maximum exposure.

Easy ways to get more videos in without the extra time is to do video interviews with people or to schedule live streams. These two types of videos take less time to prepare and edit so they can be an easy way to get an additional video out each week.

Consistency is also extremely important on YouTube. What do you think would happen if your favorite TV show aired...just whenever the producers felt like it? Some weeks it might air on Saturday, others it might be Tuesday.

I don't think even Seinfeld could have kept an audience with that kind of chaotic schedule.

Not only does YouTube want you to publish at the same day and time every week, your community wants it as well. How do you do this without missing or being late on videos?

Make a goal of being scheduled at least a week ahead on your videos. You might have to hustle at first to get out ahead but once you're going, is it really any different than doing each video at the last minute?

Make a social media plan – You don't need to share on every social platform but smaller channels aren't getting much help from YouTube so you do need a plan to get traffic from somewhere. Create a social marketing plan you use for every video and maybe an extended plan you use on videos you want to promote a little more.

- Share on Facebook, Twitter, LinkedIn and Pinterest at a minimum. These are the platforms that result in the most social traffic for my videos but yours might be different. Create images that work best for each individual platform, i.e. landscape for FB, Twitter and LinkedIn but portrait format for Pinterest.

- Make a goal of trying out a new social platform every three- or six-months and integrating it into your social marketing plan if you see views coming from the site.

- Personally ask contacts to watch and engage for your really important videos. Simply sharing on social might get you a few views but direct messages will always work better.

- Keep track of the posts and videos that get the most

engagement on social and reschedule the posts every few months to re-invigorate your older videos.

Your goal here should be to stick with a basic social marketing plan for your videos and to regularly test new ideas. Evolution is the name of the game in business. If you're not adapting to changes and progressing, you could be falling behind without even knowing it.

Testing new ideas for videos – Take that idea of constant improvement into other areas of your channel as well. Make a goal of testing new ideas at least every few months, giving each a month or two to see what works.

- Test new thumbnail formats like colors, fonts, backgrounds and whether you have your face in the image or not. You can try thumbnail ideas on new videos or replacing ones on old videos that aren't getting much traffic.

- Test out new topics in your niche or even topics outside your niche. We'll talk more about this in the chapter on content strategy but make a point to regularly browse related channels to see what is working for them.

- Test out doing live streams once a week. These take much less time to produce and can build some great engagement with your community.

Your goal here should be put these kinds of tests on your schedule and stick with it. It's easy to fall into a routine but you'll never know what you're missing unless you constantly work on new ideas.

Collaborations – Working with other creators is one of the most often cited ways to reach new viewers and boost your channel.

I've done dozens of interviews for my channel but have done fewer collaborations with other YouTube creators. This one is definitely on my list for top goals this year and beyond.

Creativity is how you'll get the most out of your collabs. That means doing different types of partnerships to give viewers something special and make a bigger impression on new audiences.

- Split-screen interviews are easy and there's no travel involved. These are probably the easiest to produce as well.

- In-person interviews seem to get more views but you'll have to coordinate travel. These work best when you're both attending a conference.

- Simply mentioning another creator's video or channel and then linking to it in the video description.

- Sharing each other's video in your Community Tab

- Hosting a video from the other creator. Create an introduction of 15- to 30-seconds to introduce the creator and what they'll be talking about and maybe a 15-second end screen for the end of the video.

- Challenge videos are a fun way to engage with other channels and don't involve any coordination. These can go viral if your challenge goes out to other channels and becomes popular; i.e. the ALS Ice Bucket Challenge or the Hot Pepper Challenge.

- Pro/Con collabs – this is a project I did with some bloggers years ago and it worked really well. You take a controversial topic, something like buying vs. renting, and each take a side of the argument. You each make a video arguing your perspective and mention the other's video as another viewpoint. This takes some coordination because you need to know what the other creator is going to say for the mention but it's a great way to create some buzz.

With any collab, make sure everyone agrees on how you're going to share the videos and where links will be included. For any kind of video exchange, make sure everyone keeps to the level of quality that viewers are used to on the channel.

Make a goal of doing at least one collaboration per month or so many in a quarter. Of course, like any of these goals, reaching it means putting in action the things that will make it possible. For collaborations, that means regularly engaging with other channels through comments and reaching out through email. It's through these relationships that you'll open up collaboration opportunities.

Sponsorships – Let's be honest, most of us are here to make money with our channels so why wouldn't some of your goals be to make more money?

Getting companies to sponsor a video or provide you with a free product is one of the best ways small channels can monetize

YouTube. Just as you can't control your view count or subscribers, you really can't control the amount of money you make but you can control the actions like reaching out to sponsors that will lead to more money.

There are a few different ways to make money with YouTube sponsorships. Pitch a few of these to companies to see which works best for you.

- Free products or services are usually the easiest to get for smaller channels since it's lower cost and commitment for the company.

- Integrated mentions are 45- to 60-second spots within the video where you talk about how the product or service fits a need. The more closely related to the video topic, the better a mention will convert. This is a common model used by podcasts.

- Reviews of a product or service are relatively easy to rank but generally get fewer views than a broader topic. They convert better though because someone looking for a review is going to be directly and immediately interested in making a purchase.

- Video series integrating the sponsor into each have worked best for me. I start with a broader topic that will bring in a large audience, integrating sponsor mentions throughout. Follow that with two more videos on progressively narrower topics. For example, for an insurance sponsorship, your first video might talk about how much insurance viewers need before a second video about picking an insurance policy and then a third video directly reviewing the sponsor company.

Your goal here is going to be researching and outreach with a number of sponsors each month. Pay attention to other channels to see where they're getting sponsorships, either looking for product reviews or mentions. You can also look to blogs and podcasts in your niche to see which companies might be open to sponsorships.

Affiliate videos – The top two sources of YouTube income for most creators are sponsorships and affiliate commissions.

Finding good affiliates to promote is similar to sponsorships, look to what other creators and bloggers are promoting. An easy way to do this is to go to blogs in your topic and look for their Resources page. It's here that they will list out and link to their best affiliates.

It's important to pitch companies for a sponsorship partnership beyond their normal affiliate terms. A lot of companies will try to get you to simply use their affiliate program without providing any kind of a base, sponsorship for your effort.

When this happens, remind them that a lot more goes into video production including extra time and costs. You can usually get a small base fee to cover these 'additional expenses' as well as using your affiliate link within the video.

Of course, some affiliates either aren't going to have a budget for sponsorships or just won't be willing to pay a base sponsorship fee. It's up to you whether you want to integrate their affiliate link into your videos. It still might be worth it if you think conversions will make enough money or if you can't find a sponsor for a related video.

Make a goal of doing a number of affiliate-related videos each month or quarter. These can be a direct review of the affiliate or just making sure you do a video in which you can naturally mention an affiliate and link to it in the description.

Super-content Videos – So I've also called these 'hack' videos but they don't necessarily need to be video ideas you get from other creators. The idea is that you want to regularly be posting videos that go beyond your normal content, videos in extremely popular topics or that go into much more detail than usual.

Your goal here might be to do at least one super-content video a month. These will take more time to produce but you're more likely to be rewarded with more views and subs.

What are your YouTube channel goals? What are the types of goals you've used to motivate you to reach that next level? What have been the goals that have best influenced your success? Finding these actions over which you have some control and creating goals around them is your best shot at driving higher views and growing your channel.

Action Steps:

- Set an email reminder for a month after starting your channel. By this point, you'll have a better idea of what you want your goals to be.

- Create multiple goals for each topic above. At least one should be shorter-term, maybe three- or six-month goals. Others can be longer-term like one-year goals.

- Goals should be difficult to reach but achievable. That difficulty will motivate you to work harder, putting the goal just within your reach.

YOUTUBE BASICS: HOW TO SET UP A YOUTUBE CHANNEL FOR SUCCESS

Learn how to set up a YouTube channel and get your message to go viral

This is going to be an easy chapter, mostly procedural for setting up your YouTube channel and getting started. I'll guide you through the basic YouTube channel setup as well as some inside secrets that will help make your channel more successful.

Resist the urge to skip through or just skim it though. It's these channel basics that will make sure the YouTube gods smile down on you and send views your way.

Besides how to start a channel on YouTube, I'll show you how to build community through the comment section, how to make money on your videos and a great way to get more subscribers from every single video.

The companion video course to the book includes a screenshare walk-through, a live step-by-step to setting up your channel. Use this link to save 35% off the course price!

Creating Your YouTube Channel

Actually starting a YouTube channel is pretty easy. Click through to YouTube and sign in with a Gmail address. If you've already signed in, you can use this menu to create a new channel.

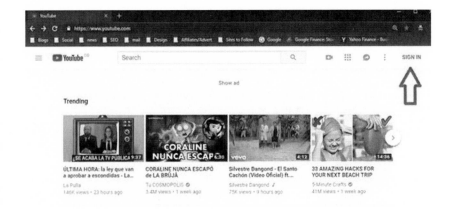

In the menu, click on the gear icon and then Create a New Channel. You'll then add your channel name.

Important tip: Creating a new channel might be too easy! Take the time to think about your channel name before you start the channel. It should be easy to remember and fit with the brand message you want to develop.

Basic YouTube Channel Setup

Once you've signed in and created a channel, you can click on your user image in the top-right corner for the channel menu. Here you can navigate to your channel, switch accounts and go to your channel dashboard by clicking on Creator Studio.

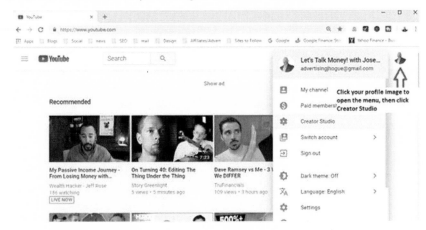

Note: We'll be working in the classic Creator Studio dashboard which is set to be deprecated in late 2019. As I write this, most of the setup

features are still not available in the new Studio beta dashboard. When everything is transitioned, the layout to the dashboard may be a little different but everything below will still apply to setting up your YouTube channel.

The first thing you see in Creator Studio will be your dashboard, a collection of menu items people use often and displayed for convenience. You can customize your dashboard by clicking in the top-right corner of each section or by clicking Add Widget.

Inside Tip: A lot of running a successful business, and this includes YouTube, is creating a quick and efficient process to your work. Take a couple of minutes to customize your dashboard to show the menu items you use most often and cut down the time it takes each day.

The first menu item will be your Video Manager, where you'll edit information about individual videos and your playlists. Setting up your channel, you won't have anything in this section, but we'll talk more about it later in uploading a video and creating playlists.

We'll also use the Live Streaming menu item in a later chapter.

Building a Community on YouTube and Responding to Comments

The Community link is where you can respond, delete or flag comments as spam. Responding to comments regularly is a great way to build a community around your channel and keep people coming back for every new video.

Within the community settings, you can add moderators to help review comments. You'll also want to hold comments that include links or hashtags so you can review them before they go public. Also check to hold potentially inappropriate chat messages for review during live streams.

Setting up your YouTube Channel and Monetization

The 'Channel' section of the menu is where we'll be making the most changes to set up your YouTube channel. The 'Status and Features' page is mostly just a heads-up display of different programs on the platform. You'll also be able to click through for more information and to access the different programs.

You're able to monetize your channel after you reach 1,000 subscribers and 4,000 watch hours in a 12-month period. Once this happens, you can click through to 'Monetization' and click to join the program. It may take a month or two for your approval to be processed.

Get that money! Setup and change monetization with this menu.

When you do get approved, you'll need to create or link a Google AdSense account to your channel for payment. You'll also want to change the settings in 'Monetization Settings for Future Videos' to change which ads show up on your channel.

Toggle the box for 'Monetize with Ads' and then select which ads you want to use.

- Overlay in-Video Ads are small banner ads that show at the bottom of your videos while playing.

- Skippable Video Ads are the pre-video ads that play.

- Non-Skippable Video Ads play through and cannot be clicked out after five seconds.

- Sponsored Cards are just like your own cards but from sponsors.

- Automatic Mid-roll Ads are skippable video ads that play during your video, like a traditional TV commercial break.

YouTube is really good at designing ad programs that aren't so annoying they turn off viewers. Users have come to expect ads when they use YouTube so you shouldn't worry too much about this, just enjoy that monthly advertising check.

That said, I've disabled non-skippable ads, sponsored cards and automatic mid-roll ads. To me, these seem especially intrusive but the choice is up to you because more ads means more money.

How to Boost YouTube Subscribers from each Video

One of my favorite features of the channel setup is under the Branding link in the menu. This allows you to place a small image in the lower-right corner of your videos. When someone hovers over the image with their mouse, a box will pop up prompting them to subscribe to your channel.

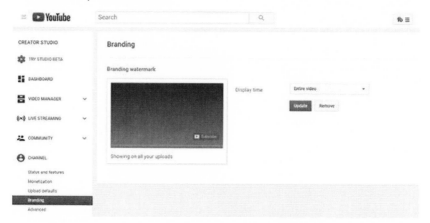

Many people still just use YouTube for how-to and for the occasional funny cat video. They don't yet see it as an alternative to TV where they can follow their favorite channels. That means you need to use every opportunity you can to ask them to subscribe and join your community.

YouTube recommends a transparent image for a watermark but I've found these don't show up very well. Don't worry about distracting viewers...that's what you want to do so use a solid image that will show up better.

You can select whether the image shows from the beginning of your video or after a certain amount of time. Select any image from your computer and upload it as your watermark.

Some channels upload a custom image for their branding watermark. I like the idea but just make sure it's clear that you want people to subscribe. I like having the traditional YouTube subscribe button so people constantly get that message. Whether they hover and click over the watermark or not, I've put the idea in their head.

Final Menu Items to Change to Set Up a YouTube Channel

Finally, you'll click through the 'Advanced' settings though there aren't many changes to make here from the default settings.

Make sure your country is selected. This affects the videos you see more than it affects the people that will see your videos.

You can also add keywords for your channel. It's not clear how much these help in search and discovery of your videos. Just like the tags you put in individual videos, these are more like suggestions on how to rank your channel and videos on the platform.

We'll spend some time talking about keyword research in a later chapter. Pick some of the larger keyword or keyword phrases that apply to your channel broadly and enter them here.

You can also link your AdWords Account here to promote your own videos. To be honest, I've yet to find an ad strategy that works better than sponsoring collaborations with other YouTubers. Users have gotten so used to ads on YouTube that they largely ignore them so you're mostly just wasting your money. I'll share a strategy for sponsoring collabs with other creators later in the book.

You can also link a website or blog to your channel to use in cards. This is a good idea to help use your channel and website together and promote products.

Last here, toggle to 'Allow my Channel to Appear in Other Channels' to turn on the featured channels area in the margin of your channel home page. It can be frustrating to see other channels featured with a clickable link on your home page but understand that your channel will also be featured on other channels (not necessarily on the same channels that are featured on your page).

YouTube changes its basic settings regularly so all of these features may not be available when you set up your channel. Spend a little time to get to know the features available and use them to set your channel up right. YouTube wants you to be successful, it wants your channel to gain subscribers. Get your channel started right and you'll be ready for success with your first videos.

HOW TO SET UP A YOUTUBE CHANNEL PAGE FOR VIRAL VIDEOS

Setting up a YouTube Channel Page takes less than half an hour and will help build community and subscribers

If you could have your own page on the world's fourth most trafficked website and the second most popular search engine... wouldn't you jump at the chance?

Of course you would!

That's why it always baffles me to see a YouTube channel page that is either not set up well or completely neglected altogether.

Setting up your YouTube channel page takes almost no time compared to creating videos and all the other things you'll do to become a YouTube star. It will help you build your brand, grow your subscriber base and make more money.

This is low-hanging fruit to getting more views...don't miss the opportunity!

How Important is Your YouTube Channel Page?

Most people watching your videos will never see your Channel page. What's more, the views from your channel page amount to an almost insignificant number.

So why worry about creating your Home page on YouTube? Is it really that important?

A lot of YouTube is about those incremental changes that build your brand, make you look like a professional and legitimate channel, and that get you just that little bit more watch-time to trigger something in the YouTube algorithm.

That's exactly what your Channel page is going to do!

Look at my traffic sources in the table below. Channel page views and those from my playlist pages account for only about 3% of the total views for my channel. That's still meant more than 15,000 views from these pages. That's fifteen thousand views that are adding to my videos' watch-time and helping them rank.

Traffic source	Watch time (minutes)	Views	YouTube Premium watch time (minutes)	YouTube Premium views	Average view duration
Browse features	3,483,321 (56%)	544,953 (54%)	200,939 (53%)	33,517 (54%)	6:23
Suggested videos	1,667,690 (27%)	264,626 (26%)	96,217 (25%)	14,752 (24%)	6:17
YouTube search	364,149 (5.8%)	67,591 (6.7%)	19,721 (5.2%)	3,299 (5.3%)	5:23
Channel pages	157,353 (2.5%)	27,996 (2.8%)	9,473 (2.5%)	1,666 (2.7%)	5:37
Other YouTube features	149,360 (2.4%)	20,626 (2.0%)	24,333 (6.4%)	3,480 (5.6%)	7:14
Direct or unknown	113,865 (1.8%)	21,087 (2.1%)	15,741 (4.1%)	2,485 (4.0%)	5:23
External	80,038 (1.3%)	21,330 (2.1%)	2,623 (0.7%)	612 (1.0%)	3:45
YouTube advertising	78,457 (1.3%)	20,411 (2.0%)	0 (0.0%)	0 (0.0%)	3:50
Notifications	61,393 (1.0%)	11,752 (1.2%)	3,251 (0.9%)	744 (1.2%)	5:13
Playlist page	47,312 (0.8%)	7,184 (0.7%)	4,016 (1.1%)	629 (1.0%)	6:35
Playlists	26,351 (0.4%)	4,401 (0.4%)	2,290 (0.6%)	397 (0.6%)	5:59
End screens	17,750 (0.3%)	2,642 (0.3%)	926 (0.2%)	165 (0.3%)	6:43
Video cards and annotations	4,127 (0.1%)	588 (0.1%)	216 (0.1%)	34 (0.1%)	7:01

Not only that, but average view duration from these sources tends to be longer than many others. Those incremental views might just be enough to trigger something in the YouTube algorithm and put your video in more search and suggested results.

So a spectacular YouTube Home page isn't going to take your channel to one million subs alone but it will help. Creating a professional-looking and interesting channel page is going to help build your brand and drive community engagement, two things no channel can be successful without.

If you still need convincing, while casual viewers might not be looking at your channel home page, you better believe that anyone thinking of sponsoring your channel will be looking!

How to Create the Best Channel Header Art

Your YouTube channel art is the first thing people see on your page and your first shot at creating an impression for your brand.

You do this with images and text that reveal branding, what your channel offers viewers and information.

- Include a slogan or mission, preferably something you repeat in videos, to start building that top-of-mind messaging.
- Tell people to subscribe and when new videos are posted

- Use imaging that evokes emotions and the brand identity you want to build

You'll add links to the bottom of your About Page that you can show on your channel art in the lower-right corner. The first should be a subscribe link to your channel. You can link out to your blogs or other sites if you like but try to keep people on YouTube to start.

I've found Fiverr is great for projects like creating channel art. For $5 each, you can get several ideas from different freelancers and choose the best for your channel. Don't be afraid to ask for revisions and ask for a few different formats you can use on different social platforms, i.e. different sizes of your channel art.

How to Create an About Page on YouTube

Like so many opportunities on YouTube, the About Page is too often missed. I cry a little inside when I visit an About Page on a friend's channel and it's completely blank.

Your About Page is another opportunity to build your brand, grow community and give YouTube signals for its algorithm. Why would you NOT take advantage of that?!?

You're limited to how much you can write here so it's prime real estate.

- The first lines on your About Page will show up when your channel appears in a search so make these a strong pitch for why people should click through.
- Use your best channel keywords throughout the description.
- Use your description to enforce branding messages like shared beliefs and common enemies, anything you can do to bring people into the community.

- Tell people what your channel is about and why they MUST be a part of your community.
- Share your qualifications and some personal information to reach people on a closer level.

At the bottom of the About Page, you'll have the chance to add links. These can be to your blog, email capture landing pages, sales pages, just about anything. You can also designate which show up as clickable links on your Home page.

Should You Turn on Featured Channels on YouTube?

You can turn on the Featured Channels column that will appear in the right sidebar to your YouTube channel page. This is done by clicking Customize Channel and mousing over the right sidebar.

This area is a good opportunity to promote other YouTube channels you own or with which you partner. I turned mine off recently but may turn it back on if I start partnering more with others. This might be a good opportunity to Collab with others, sharing links to each other's channel in your Featured Channels space.

Should You Show Related Channels on YouTube?

The Related Channels sidebar appears under Featured Channels and is turned on when you set up your channel settings.

This will almost always display channels with a higher following than yours and it's difficult to really know if it's doing your channel any good. Presumably by turning this on, you're also being displayed in the sidebar of other channels though there is no way of knowing which unless you happen to find them by luck.

Still, sidebar click-through-rates are not very high so I wouldn't worry about losing viewers to the channels displayed in this section. YouTube likes it when you help promote other channels and I have to think that they reward channels that turn on this feature.

How to Get the Most from YouTube Playlists

Playlists are one of the most important features of a YouTube channel and too often missed by beginners. A playlist is a grouping of videos by theme, process or really whatever you want it to be.

When someone clicks through to a playlist, all the videos will play automatically in succession. This is a great way to keep people on your channel, grow watch-time and build loyalty in your community.

Anyone that watches three of your videos in a row is going to subscribe and be a part of your community. At this point, you've appeared enough times that they feel like they know you and trust your content.

Not only do playlists keep people watching your channel, they also...

- Adding a video to a playlist creates a totally new URL which is like a signal to YouTube of new content
- Playlist views tend to have longer average view duration
- Videos in a playlist are more likely to show up as suggested videos for each other

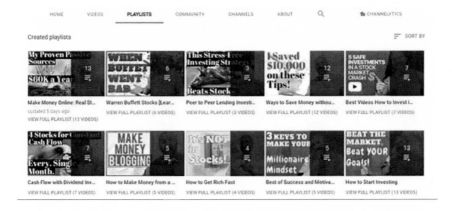

Starting a new playlist on YouTube takes less than a couple of minutes. You can go through the Studio in Video Manager or click Customize Channel within the playlists tab and add a new playlist title.

From within the new playlist, click to add a description and add videos.

Make sure you include keyword-rich titles and descriptions to your playlists. Just as with individual videos, good titles and descriptions will increase your click-through-rate and tell YouTube which keywords are important to rank for your playlist.

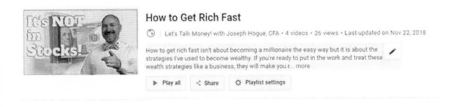

How to Get Rich Fast

Let's Talk Money! with Joseph Hogue, CFA • 4 videos • 26 views • Last updated on Nov 22, 2018

How to get rich fast isn't about becoming a millionaire the easy way but it is about the strategies I've used to become wealthy. If you're ready to put in the work and treat these wealth strategies like a business, they will make you r... more

▶ Play all   ◁ Share   ⚙ Playlist settings

From within your playlist, there are a few settings you can change,

- Auto Add videos depending on keywords. I generally don't use this preferring instead to manage it myself.

- Collaborate will let other channels add videos and is a great way to collaborate. Remember, the algorithm rewards channels that lead viewers to long session watch-times so don't be afraid to share great content from others.

- Set as Official Series will make it more likely that videos within the playlist appear as suggested videos when each is viewed outside the playlist. Videos in an official series can't be used in another playlist though.

- Allow embedding – always allow embedding on your videos…why not give people the opportunity to share your videos anywhere?

- Ordering the videos in your playlist. I keep this on manual but 'most popular' is also a good choice. Unless the videos need to be in a specific order, you want your best and highest-converting to show up first.

I generally wait a week or two after publication to add new videos to a playlist. This gives them time to get views and then that extra boost when a new playlist URL is created.

You should also be adding older videos to playlists regularly and creating new playlists. Creating a new playlist or adding a video to one is like a signal of new content to YouTube. Do this one or two days a week when you're not publishing a new video and YouTube will see your channel as more consistent and frequent with your content.

Just as with your regular publishing schedule, I recommend adding an old video to a playlist or creating a new list the same day and time each week.

How to Use the YouTube Community Tab on Your Channel

If I cry a little when I see a neglected About Page, I absolutely die when I see a YouTube channel not taking advantage of its Community Tab!

The Community Tab used to be available only to channels with 10,000+ subscribers but recently got unlocked for those with 1K subs or more. It's an amazing feature so send in a support request asking for it if your channel hasn't been approved yet.

There are so many opportunities here from building community to keeping subscribers engaged when you aren't able to publish a video. Engagement with community posts makes it more likely people will see your videos and you can get some great information through polls.

You can also use the tab to build excitement for upcoming videos and get incremental views for older ones. Even on a smaller channel, I can drive a few hundred clicks to a video by creating a community tab post. That can be enough to juice the YouTube algorithm and get more organic views.

Some ways you should be using community tab

- Motivational quotes to build community
- Polls get great engagement and can get you excellent information about subscribers
- Show your personal side with behind-the-scenes to build community
- Clicks to your videos through video posts
- Build excitement for an upcoming video

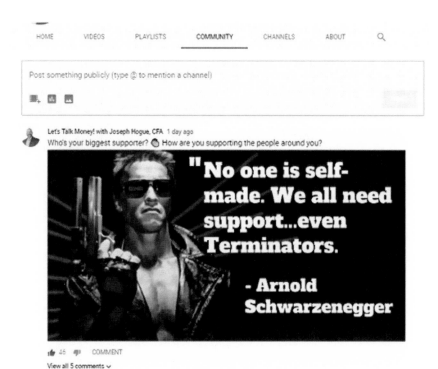

You can share YouTube videos, images, polls or gifs in your community tab. YouTube recently launched a feature allowing you to tag other channels, a great way to let others know you're promoting them.

Should You Make a Channel Welcome Video?

You can designate a video to show up to non-subscribers that land on your channel page. The conventional wisdom is to create a special welcome video of 30 – 90 seconds, kind of like a commercial for your channel.

This is intuitive and a great way to quickly tell new visitors what your channel is about. I've seen some really great welcome videos... and unfortunately a lot of really bad ones as well.

I actually prefer a different strategy, showing your highest-converting video in this spot. While this might not convey everything you want new visitors to know about your channel, there are some benefits including not having to make a new video and the ability to use a proven video to convert subs. I've also experimented with the idea of changing this feature video to the most recent published, helping to build that initial watch-time for new videos.

If you do go with a channel welcome video,

- Make it brief, no longer than 90-seconds.
- Make it high-energy and exciting. This might be your first impression with a visitor, evoke those emotions and the energy that will convince them to subscribe.
- Tell visitors exactly who should describe and maybe even who should not subscribe. This kind of honesty and exclusivity helps build the kind of trust that builds a community.
- Tell visitors why they should subscribe, what you talk about and how it will benefit them.

How to Set up Horizontal Playlists on Your YouTube Channel Page

You have the option of showing videos or playlists horizontally or vertically on your YouTube channel page. I like horizontal because it shows more videos and just seems to make better use of the space.

Either way you choose, it's best to keep it consistent so don't make some sections horizontal and others vertical.

To set this up, click Customize Channel and choose what type of content you want in each section. You can move sections around by mousing over the little downward arrow and dragging.

I like to start with the most recent uploads so subscribers can quickly find new content. I'll then add sections for popular videos and playlists.

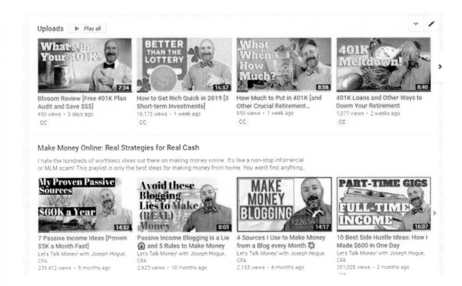

Uploads ▶ Play all

Bloom Review [Free 401K Plan Audit and Save $$$]
450 views • 5 days ago
CC

How to Get Rich Quick in 2019 [3 Short-term Investments]
16,173 views • 1 week ago
CC

How Much to Put in 401K [and Other Crucial Retirement...
959 views • 1 week ago
CC

401K Loans and Other Ways to Doom Your Retirement
1,077 views • 2 weeks ago
CC

Make Money Online: Real Strategies for Real Cash

I hate the hundreds of worthless ideas out there on making money online. It's like a non-stop infomercial or MLM scam! This playlist is only the best ideas for making money from home. You won't find anything...

7 Passive Income Ideas [Proven $5K a Month Fast]
Let's Talk Money! with Joseph Hogue, CFA
239,412 views • 8 months ago

Passive Income Blogging is a Lie and 5 Rules to Make Money
Let's Talk Money! with Joseph Hogue, CFA
2,623 views • 10 months ago

4 Sources I Use to Make Money from a Blog every Month
Let's Talk Money! with Joseph Hogue, CFA
2,133 views • 6 months ago

10 Best Side Hustle Ideas: How I Made $600 in One Day
Let's Talk Money! with Joseph Hogue, CFA
201,028 views • 2 months ago

It might seem like a lot to set up your YouTube Channel Page but all this will only take a few hours at most. You might go back and change a few of the settings or revise your About Page occasionally but most of these will never change. Against hundreds of millions of active YouTube channels, you need every point you can get to grow your brand and build community. Don't neglect one of the easiest ways to make your channel look professional and earn subscribers.

Action Steps:

- Use some of the niche ideas we talked about and brainstorm things you want to say on your About Page. We'll also use elements of branding from a later chapter.

- List a few playlists you can make when you start uploading videos. This kind of planning means you'll be creating videos in a specific theme and really keep viewers hooked to watch them all.

HOW TO HACK YOUTUBE FOR VIDEO IDEAS

Getting great YouTube video ideas is more than just making videos around your topic, it's about the research to find ideas that go viral

So you've started a YouTube channel, you've put in hours setting up your page and thinking through branding. You've got your video equipment set up and you're ready to go.

Now, there's just one problem...what should you make videos about???

It seems there would be an obvious answer, make videos around your niche. Just start making videos that you think your audience will want to watch...but not so fast.

With over 300 hours of video uploaded to YouTube every minute, you need more than just a quick video idea to compete. Your video content strategy needs to be just that...strategic.

This means research to find the YouTube video ideas that get views. Just 15 minutes of research and SEO can mean all the difference and I'm going to show you exactly how to do it.

How to Find Video Ideas to Get as Many Views as Possible on YouTube

Just like with Google search, video views on YouTube revolve around keywords. It's your video's ranking for keywords that determines where it shows up in search and suggested videos. These are going to be two of the biggest traffic sources for your videos so it's important to find the keywords that will drive views.

Also like Google though, you can't just create a video around a high-volume keyword. Create a video around the keyword 'make money online' and you'll be buried under millions of other videos. The keyword might get over 70,000 searches a month but you'll need some serious watch-time to rank for it.

Instead, you'll need to find keywords with a high search-volume but that have lower competition from other creators. You'll take that broad, highly-searched keyword and find related keywords by adding a few more words.

There are two methods I use to research keywords and YouTube video ideas that every new creator should know; using keyword research tools and the video-hacking method.

How to Keyword Research on YouTube

I'll show you the video-hacking method next but let's start with basic keyword research that accounts for the majority of my video ideas on YouTube.

I use two tools for keyword research, the Keywords Everywhere plugin and TubeBuddy.

Keywords Everywhere is a free browser addon for Chrome or Firefox that shows you search volume and cost-per-click rates when searching on Google or YouTube. This allows you to see actual monthly search volume for a keyword, on the search term and any suggested terms.

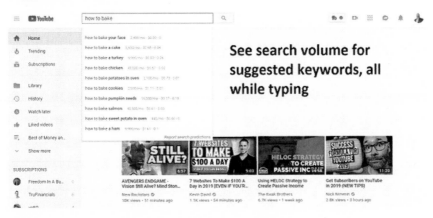

See search volume for suggested keywords, all while typing

Start with a broad keyword idea that you think will be popular and type it in the YouTube search box

- Suggestions for video ideas will auto-populate in the drop-down with the monthly search volume next to each
- Work through the alphabet, typing your main keyword

plus 'a' then 'b' and so on, looking at what appears and the search volume for each

- For smaller channels, a good place to start is keywords with between 500 to 1,000 searches but note any keywords with more than 500 searches for more research
- You can also try working through the alphabet with additional words before the main keyword, so typing 'a' then 'b' before your broad keyword
- Try adjectives before your main keyword, words like 'best, fast, easy' to see what is suggested and the search volume

Remember, you're looking for long-tail variations on your broad keyword. These are still going to have solid search volume but will not be as difficult to rank as that main idea.

With the list of potential keyword variations, I use the TubeBuddy extension to find the ones with the least amount of competition and the highest traffic.

After installing the free TubeBuddy tool, you'll find a Keyword Score that combines search volume and competition any time you search on YouTube. In the right sidebar, TubeBuddy shows you this Keyword Score as well as related searches and most used tags in results.

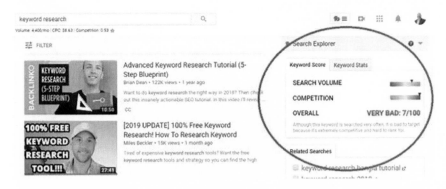

Grow your YouTube channel and you'll eventually be able to rank for competitive keywords but you'll want to start with keywords and video ideas with a score of 30 or higher at first.

For example, the broad keyword 'high paying jobs' gets over 90,000 searches a month on YouTube but has a 'poor' overall keyword score of 12 from TubeBuddy. Channels ranking for the keyword have subscriber counts in the hundreds of thousands and tens of thousands of views on the ranked video.

It's not likely many channels will be able to compete here.

On the other hand, the keyword 'high paying jobs without a degree' still gets over 3,200 searches a month and a TubeBuddy keyword score of 30 or 'fair'. One video ranking for the keyword has just 265 views and channels with just a few thousand subs are ranking.

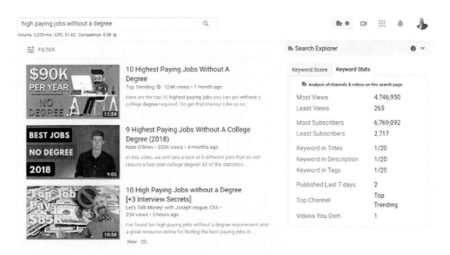

TubeBuddy also has a Keyword Explorer tool that helps find suggestions for video ideas. Open the TubeBuddy platform and click to the explorer. You'll see the keyword score for any search term as well as related and trending results.

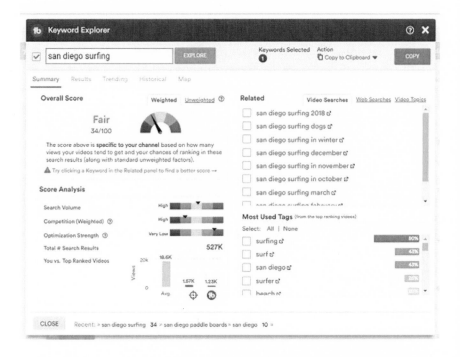

Remember, while you want to find keyword variations with solid search volume, don't sacrifice ranking or a high Keyword Score just to target a video idea with thousands of search traffic. It does you no good to rank 20th for a high-traffic keyword when you could rank in the top five for a smaller keyword and get legit views.

Aim for those keywords for which you can rank and get steady views. Over time, those views will contribute to the video watch-time and the overall watch-time for your channel. That's what it takes to grow on YouTube. Growing your watch-time to rank for more competitive keywords.

Video Hacking to Find Viral Keywords on YouTube

While researching keywords comes up with the majority of my YouTube video ideas, there's another strategy I use that has produced some of my biggest hits.

It's called video-hacking and it's a much more straight-forward way to getting viral video ideas.

Whereas keyword research feels like you're starting from scratch, finding a good keyword and creating content, video-hacking starts you off with ideas that are already proven winners.

Start by finding five YouTube channels similar to yours. These should be popular channels but not necessarily ones with millions of subscribers. The idea here is to find channels with some really popular videos, with views in the hundreds of thousands, but not channels that will rank for anything by virtue of their size.

I've found the best targets for this video-hacking idea are channels with between 50k to 250k subscribers.

For each of the five target channels, go to 'Videos' and sort by popularity. Then list the title of the top five or ten videos in a spreadsheet.

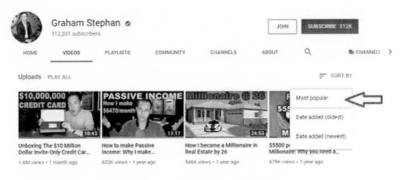

Since having the keyword in the title is so important for YouTube, the main keyword is probably going to be in the title for each of the videos in your list. You can also click through to the videos and see which keywords they're ranking by using the TubeBuddy extension.

Once you've got a list of the most viewed videos for each of your target channels, you're going to start seeing overlap. There will be keywords that are popular across all the channels, keywords that get massive views for everyone in the niche.

Pick out at least three or four of these winning video ideas and get ready to make a viral video!

To compete with some of these bigger channels, we're going to be using an old blogging technique called the 'skyscraper approach'. The strategy, attributed to Brian Dean of Backlinko, involves searching your keyword on YouTube and Google to brainstorm everything that needs to be in an epic video.

Do a search for your keyword:

- Click through and note the main topics and ideas that are covered in the first five or ten search results, these are usually revealed in the section headings for articles
- Note the 'People Also Ask' suggestions in a Google search
- Note the 'Searches Related to…' at the bottom of the Google search
- Note the talking points and anything unique in YouTube video results

These are all ideas that both Google and YouTube feel relate closely to the keyword and need to be in any content that ranks. Your goal in creating epic content is going to be to create a 'super-video' that incorporates as much as possible.

The Skyscraper is more than just copying down what other people are saying. You'll want to research and find the detail others missed and put your video together in a way that keeps people watching in its entirety.

Don't forget to add graphics, personal stories, branding and all the other things that keep people watching and engaged with your video.

While you're looking at the top results for the keyword on YouTube, check out the titles and thumbnails as well. You'll need to create something special and different from the existing content to get noticed so you might want to brainstorm your title ideas and thumbnails now while it's top-of-mind.

Produce five or more of these video-hacking YouTube ideas and I guarantee they'll blow your other videos away in terms of views and it's likely at least one will become a most-viewed video for your channel.

Running with Your Winners on YouTube

Finding a strong keyword or one that's worked for other channels doesn't automatically mean it's going to get viral views. There are reportedly millions of factors that go into the YouTube discovery algorithm so even finding keywords that work well for peer channels, sometimes it all seems like a crap shoot.

But spend just ten minutes to do your keyword and video idea research and you will have winners.

It's here where you have the chance to really grow your channel.

When you do have a winning video, we're talking a video that blows all your others away and gets 100K+ views, take the broader keyword from the video and develop it into your content strategy.

This means taking that broader keyword and finding at least four to six long-tail variations on it for more videos. This will create a library of videos around that topic, each detailing a more specific but related area.

The idea here is that YouTube now sees your channel as an authority on that core keyword with the successful video. Any videos you make around that will cumulatively add watch-time to the keyword authority you have on the channel and will help each rank. Each of the videos will also show up in the suggested videos for each other so you'll have that power video sending traffic to the others for instant organic ranking.

For example, if you have a video titled 'Best Jobs for College Students',

- Keyword themes here might be something like best jobs, high-paying jobs, or college students.
- Brainstorm other video ideas that include these themes for example; Best Jobs for High School Students, High-Paying Jobs without a Degree, Credit Cards for College Students
- Research each long-tail variation of your keywords to find the ones with good volume and low search then produce four or five videos around the keywords

It helps to publish these follow-on videos as soon as possible to the success of your previous video. All the people that watched your viral video will be shown the new videos in their suggested and in the browser, especially the ones that 'Liked' or commented on the video.

Growing a YouTube channel is about more than just producing content. Getting great YouTube video ideas takes time and research but your effort will be rewarded. Spend just 10 or 15 minutes researching your topic ideas and keywords before filming and you'll boost views with keywords you can actually rank.

Action Steps:

- List out five to ten channels similar to yours and create a spreadsheet listing their top ten videos by views. Look for common titles and keywords across the channels.

- Create a spreadsheet for YouTube keyword research. Research main topic keywords in your niche and related variations of each. Note the search volume and difficulty score for each to start getting ideas for videos you can rank.

THE ULTIMATE YOUTUBE EQUIPMENT CHECKLIST [AND HOW TO USE IT]

What equipment you need to get started on YouTube and how to use it for viral views

One of the great things about YouTube is that you can get started with just the phone in your pocket. What a time we live in that everyone has a mini-video studio with them at all times.

But that also means if you want your YouTube videos to stand out, they need a professional look you're not going to get on just an iPhone.

Making YouTube a business means you need the right equipment and need to know how to use it. It's not going to be costless but the investment will pay off with a channel that grows faster.

Your investment WILL pay off.

I've put just over $1,500 in equipment and software for my YouTube channel since getting started last year. In that time, I've made over $30,000 in ads plus tens of thousands in sponsorships and affiliate sales.

That's a return on investment you'll never get from the stock market!

I'm going to detail all the equipment you need to get started on YouTube, the camera gear and software. I'll show you the equipment I use as well as some gear I think is a better choice.

Finally, I'm going to walk you through how to set up your equipment and share the tips I wish I knew when getting started.

What YouTube Equipment Do You Absolutely Need?

Understand we're not talking about the bare minimum equipment you need to start a YouTube channel. You can launch your channel with a smartphone and nothing else, just recording and uploading from your phone.

That's not the kind of setup that makes for a professional-looking channel.

You wouldn't start a professional catering business using nothing but a microwave and a hotplate. Don't think a simple smartphone is going to give your videos the look they need to get views.

I'll talk through the equipment I use and some options to get started. After the equipment list, I'll detail how to set everything up as well as some tips I've picked up along the way.

The first thing you're going to need is a good camera, maybe a DSLR camera which shoots high-quality digital video. I understand you can do everything on your smartphone but it just doesn't look the same.

Get off the smartphone and give your videos that professional look.

This is the one point I'm going to recommend something other than what I use. I use a Canon Rebel T6 which is a low-cost camera and shoots great video but will only film for 12 minutes before the file size gets too large.

Instead, I'd recommend the newer model DSLR cameras like the Canon 70D. This one will shoot for 30 minutes continuously and is still an economical option. The camera is really easy to use and I'll walk you through how to set it up for your YouTube videos later in the book.

One of the best pieces of YouTube equipment you can buy is a digital recorder, I use the Zoom H4N Pro. The audio you get through your computer camera or even a DSLR just isn't great quality. YouTube viewers will give you a pass if your video image is a little grainy but your audio quality needs to be excellent. Using a separate digital recorder creates crystal-clear audio for your videos.

Along with the digital recorder, I also use a lapel microphone like this one from PowerdeWise. With Lav Mics, you don't need to go expensive and can get one for $30 or less.

I know some YouTubers like to use a camera-mounted microphone or one above their heads on a boom. These can work but if there's the slightest bit of background noise, they'll pick up on it. With a lav mic, you get only the sound you want and can use it in any situation.

You'll also need a camera tripod for steady shots and almost every YouTube channel I know uses the Amazon Basics 60-inch tripod. It's not as solid as some of the more expensive models but it's a great option to get started.

Editing software is another one I'll suggest something different than I use for YouTube. I use Camtasia to edit my YouTube videos. It's a good program and easy to use but there are some bugs that can get annoying and you miss out on some of the functionality you get from other video editing software.

It's a little more expensive but the standard for video editing is really Adobe Premiere Pro. Not only can you do all your video editing here, you can also use it to create great thumbnails.

One of the best things you can buy for your YouTube videos is a teleprompter like the Caddie Buddy. Now a lot of people think using a teleprompter is cheating but this is going to save you hours of filming and editing time.

I don't know what it is. I can talk for hours about investing and personal finance but get me in front of a camera, trying to hit specific points and I completely forget what I wanted to say. Scripting out my videos and using a teleprompter means I can record and edit in half the time it would take to work from bullet points.

This is another piece of YouTube equipment that will take some playing around with so I've got some pointers later in the book to get you started.

Most teleprompters will work with a tablet or smartphone, reflecting what's on your screen onto the teleprompter glass. I would highly recommend getting a 10" tablet for this to give you a bigger viewing space. I started with a 7" tablet and the change to a larger one was amazing. If you're only using the tablet for your YouTube videos, you don't need much, just a simple 10" Lenovo Tablet is what I use.

One of the best pieces of equipment you can buy is an AC adapter for your camera (I use this one but make sure you get one compatible with your camera). This, along with the teleprompter, is another one that has cut hours off the time it takes to film videos.

I bought a replacement battery for my camera before I got an AC adapter. Even with the two batteries, I was still constantly changing out batteries and having to wait for one to recharge before filming. I almost missed out on some great interviews at a conference because my batteries were dead. Being able to just plug in your camera to continuous power will save you time and a lot of stress.

Good lighting is one of the best ways to set your YouTube videos apart from all the other channels. Too many creators think they can just flip on the light switch and make a video.

Great lighting means lighting your face or subject with no shadows and understanding sunlight-type soft light.

I know a lot of YouTube creators swear by a ring light, which is easy to set up and provides good lighting. I prefer to use a traditional three-point photography setup like this one from Emart. This setup lets you position the lights to remove all shadows and you can use the smaller light to brighten your backdrop.

Along with the umbrella lights, you'll need bulbs that are 5500K or higher. This is something a lot of creators don't know about, that lights are measured by a level of Kelvin that determines the type of light. Your average room bulbs are around 3000K which is incandescent lighting color.

Sunlight and the bulbs that recreate it more closely, are those with a Kelvin of 5500 or higher. Use anything lower or forget to turn off your room lights when filming, and your video could have a yellowish-color.

I do most of my videos on the DSLR camera but use a Logitech C920 for interviews and any kind of webinar or computer-based videos. This is the webcam you'll see almost everyone else using and provides quality 1080 HD video.

You'll also need memory cards for your camera and the digital recorder. I use 64 GB cards but that's probably more than you need because I've never gotten even close to the storage limit. These are low-cost YouTube equipment though so might as well get more than you need so you can use it for years.

Our last piece of must-have YouTube equipment is a grey card for adjusting the white balance on your camera. I used the automatic white balance feature on my camera for a long time until I realized just how much better the color-quality is when you do it yourself. I'll show you how to set it up below.

What YouTube Equipment is a Good to Have?

Besides the must-have equipment to get started, there are a couple of things you can buy that will give you a little extra quality and stress-free recording. Most of these are fairly low-cost so won't set you back much but you might want to wait before you make the extra commitment.

One of the most recent pieces of equipment I've bought is a hair light on a boom arm. This light goes behind you and shines down on the back of your head and shoulders. This highlights your body and really separates it from the background.

You'll be surprised how much a difference this will make in your videos. You can also buy a light panel that attaches to the wall behind you but I like the boom arm setup for its flexibility.

If you want to do white background or greenscreen videos, you'll need a studio backdrop stand on which you can drape cloth or paper canvas. I use a 10' adjustable stand that also acts to hold my paper lanterns for interview and webinar videos.

If you're doing an interview on your computer or just don't want to set up your full lighting setup, these paper globe lights are a great alternative. Put in a 5500K soft bulb and they'll spread the light evenly all around. I hang two from my backdrop stand, one on each side of my face and about two feet in front, for interviews. They aren't quite as focused as the umbrella lights but are cheap and quick to put together.

Doing live interviews, you can either hook each person up to a lav mic or just use an omnidirectional hand-held microphone. The mic will connect directly to your digital recorder to capture quality sound without the background noise. It will also enable you to interview more than one person at a time and without having to mic everyone up with a lav mic.

If you're going to be moving around or doing vlogger videos then you'll need a good hand-held tripod like the Gorillapod by JOBY. This tripod is strong enough to handle your DSLR camera and extremely flexible to position however you want it.

How to Set Up and Use Your YouTube Equipment

I'm not going to spend a lot of time on the mechanics of setting up your YouTube equipment. All of it's pretty easy to hook up. What I do want to show you are all the inside tricks you won't get from an instruction manual.

Most of these are tips I had to learn the hard way, through mistakes and trial-and-error.

Lighting is relatively easy to set up. At a minimum, you want two umbrella lights or soft boxes in front of you. You'll hear a lot of technical terms and rules for positioning but you don't necessarily need to get into the details here.

The graphic shows the traditional three-point lighting with two lights in front and one hair-light in back. A photography-freak would tell you the Key Light needs to be brighter but I've never found that it makes a difference. I position both the front lights at about 45 degree angles to me to take out all the shadows on my face.

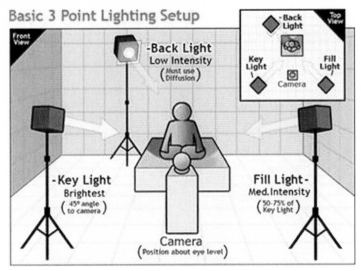

Basic 3 Point Lighting Setup

Don't be afraid to play around a little with the height of your lights or the angle of the umbrellas. What is important here is that your face is well-lit with no shadows so just adjust your lights until you get it.

Watch for any glare from your lights onto pictures or screens in the background as well.

Connecting the lav mic with your Zoom H4N recorder and getting started is fairly easy. Instead of clipping the lav mic to the outside of your shirt, you might try taping it to the inside. Use a single piece of tape that completely covers the microphone to tape it to the inside of your shirt, about halfway between your nipples and your mouth.

When you're using the digital recorder, you have to press the REC button twice to start recording. The first few times you use the device, make it a point to double-check that the time indicator is running and that you're recording. That's going to build the habit of checking it and save you a lot of time and frustration.

It's only happened once but getting ten minutes into recording a video before realizing you only touched the REC button once, and it's not recording your audio, can ruin your whole day!

Remember to tap the REC button twice to start recording!

Using the teleprompter is where I've made the most mistakes...err, learned the most lessons.

You'll download a teleprompter app on your tablet to reflect onto the camera screen. Most of these apps are the same and I've never seen a difference between the paid and free apps. I use the 'Simple Teleprompter' app which is free but I know the Parrot app is popular as well.

Using the teleprompter, it's crucial that you stand at least five feet from the camera. Anything less and it's going to be obvious you're reading...and you'll hear about it in the comments. Don't worry too much about these comments if you get them, these trolls usually haven't even tried doing their own videos so what do they know.

But if your videos do appear that you're reading, it's probably that you're not far enough from the camera.

You can adjust the settings on your teleprompter app and need to spend some time testing to get it just right for your speaking speed. The slowest scroll speed was still too fast for me and I spent months just pausing and scrolling the screen manually...which meant a lot of time editing.

When I actually looked into the app settings, it was like angels singing! I adjusted the font size to 75 so I could see the text easier from farther away, something made easier by a larger tablet and helped to hide my reading eye movement. I also increased the spacing between lines to slow down the movement of the script. Clicking AutoStart and Delay will give you time to get ready before the scroll starts.

Whereas it used to take about twice the video length to record, now I can talk straight through and it saves hours editing.

The Amazon Basics Tripod has three tightening knobs at the top, where the camera or teleprompter connects. Two of these are fairly obvious but the third, the camera tilt, isn't as obvious. This was one of my duh-moments realizing that this knob tightened to keep the camera tilt locked-in.

I'm going to admit that I know very little about photography and using a camera so am going to link here to a great post on setting up your DSLR camera for videos. The most important points are setting up the ISO and adjusting the white balance. I used the automatic white balance on my camera when starting out and was amazed at the change in color quality when learning how to set it myself.

The YouTube equipment you need isn't expensive but it's critical to setting yourself apart from the thousands of creators that start every day. You can get all the equipment you need for less than $2,000 to make professional-quality videos and make many times that in ads, sponsorships and affiliate commissions.

5 STEPS TO BRANDING ON YOUTUBE AND BUILDING A COMMUNITY

Building a brand on YouTube is your best opportunity to create a community of support and grow your business

Ever wonder why some channels on YouTube seem to get hundreds of comments on every video? Is there a reason why some channels with subscriber counts in the hundreds of thousands get just a few hundred views per video while a smaller channel can consistently get thousands of views each video?

It's all in developing a community and a brand around your channel.

And if you're ever in doubt of the power of community, try commenting with anything even remotely in disagreement with something Dave Ramsey says on one of his videos...you will be torn to shreds!

Brand building is one of the best opportunities you have to growing your channel, partly for the fact that so many channels neglect it.

To be honest, I've never been good at branding my blogs or using my personality to write something that builds a community around the websites. Something is different about YouTube though.

YouTube opens up a whole new world of branding, of building a community combining visual and audible elements. Learn how to use the opportunity and you'll create an army of cheerleaders that will support and follow you in everything you do.

What is Branding and Why it Matters on YouTube

Branding is the message people get when they see your product or even think about your company. Some branding is obvious like a slogan while other messages may be almost sub-conscious.

Your brand is important for two very important reasons:

- It sells your product or service. If people see your company as a quality provider that shares their values, they're more likely to trust your sales message.

- It creates an army of cheerleaders. Your brand creates a community that will happily spread the message and support you.

There are two things to remember when thinking about how you're going to build your brand, the message you want to deliver and how you're going to deliver it.

We'll spend most of the time talking about the message you want to develop but spend a little time in each section thinking about how you can deliver that message including through visual cues, written word and video.

Delivering the same message in different formats will not only reach a wider audience but it will also reinforce your message for people that see it in different forms.

What's Your Brand?

Your brand isn't just about the quality of your product or the immediate needs it satisfies. Your brand should encompass deeper values and benefits.

Brand Example: At a cursory glance, Coca-Cola is just a soft drink. A carbonated, sugary beverage that tastes good and satisfies your thirst. Branding it around that idea might be enough to sell a lot of bottles but it wouldn't create a $215 billion international powerhouse.

When you think about Coca-Cola, I bet you think of a lot more than just those basic ideas. You might think of happiness, smiling, you might even think of Christmas.

The company has created these associations through branding for over 130 years and sells more than 1.9 billion servings a day because of it. From slogans like "Open Happiness," and a consistent marketing message, Coca-Cola has associated the drink with these emotions and triggers that make you think of the company.

Brainstorming the brand you want to build isn't a five-minute task or something you can do once and be done. Give yourself some time to really think about the message you want people to get when they think about your company but don't be afraid to let your brand evolve. Coca-Cola has used more than 40 official slogans and countless commercials in its history.

- What's the brand message around products or channels similar to yours? What do you think about when you see their commercials or content?
- What are the most obvious benefits from using your product or watching your channel?
- Looking beyond those obvious benefits, what are the deeper needs satisfied like happiness, belonging or security?
- What do you want people to think of and feel when they see your company or product?

Developing Your Brand on YouTube

YouTube is an excellent medium to develop your brand because it brings together so many ways to deliver your message; through your words, visual cues and even through a music track.

We'll spend the rest of this chapter on five components of developing your brand, ways of creating that message for potential customers. These five components can be used on any medium whether it be a blog, YouTube channel or a podcast.

Sharing Your Creation Story

Every superhero needs a creation story. It makes them more human and helps people empathize with the hero. It also breaks down any initial cynicism as to why the hero is helping people. The creation story provides an easy reason to trust the hero and their actions.

A creation story isn't just for comic books either. How many stories have you heard about the early lives of George Washington, Abraham Lincoln or other famous people?

The greatness we see in some people seems so far from our own lives that these tales help humanize them.

But you don't have to be bitten by a radioactive spider to have a great creation story. Even the most normal routine of our daily lives can be spun into a creation story that makes your greatness relatable.

- Work backwards from the message you want people to get or the shared beliefs of the community you want to build. What in your past has helped you develop those beliefs?
- What have been the major turning points in your life?
- What are the points you've experienced pain or hardship in your life? How did you come out of the experience as a better person?

My creation story involves lessons I learned in the Marine Corps and mistakes I've made with my money. My time serving in the military developed a sense of duty and integrity to serve. The mistakes I made with money early in my life and the mistakes I saw my parents make affected me deeply and at an emotional level. It's the memory of those emotions that guides me in helping people avoid them by making good financial decisions.

What are the Community's Shared Beliefs?

Shared beliefs are what binds a community together. These are deep values that mean more to your community than anything else, ideas that are bigger than any single person.

Beliefs and values are generally rather vague concepts like patriotism, honesty, loyalty, respect, the value of hard work and adventure-seeking. The ideas are pervasive enough that you don't have to define them. Everyone's definition of each might be a little different but the overall idea and feeling is the same.

It's through your community's shared beliefs that will help each individual relate to you and the rest of the community. Not only will this give them a sense of belongingness to the community but members will feel compelled to protect the community against threats.

- Beliefs and values need to be broad enough to be shared by many but exclusive enough that they aren't held by everyone.
- Shared beliefs don't necessarily need to be anything related to your product or service. Is there anything really tying

Coca-Cola and Christmas together other than the company's brand messaging?

- If you know your target customer, what are the beliefs and values shared within their culture or common experiences within their demographic?

Your creation story helps relate how you developed your own set of beliefs. Sharing this story, visual cues and other experiences will help associate your brand with these beliefs.

For example, the backdrop for my videos includes a picture of the Statue of Liberty, my shadowbox with my rank insignia and other effects from military service. The banner to my YouTube channel shows the slogan, "Creating the Financial Future You Deserve."

What are my beliefs that I'm trying to display here?

Patriotism and service are easy ones but also a sense of loyalty and trust. I'm also hoping to attract people to the community with a sense of entitlement in their financial well-being.

Using Rituals to Develop a Brand

Rituals are a fun way of building community and developing your brand. These are consistent acts, slogans or behaviors you associate with your product.

Of course, you're no stranger to rituals. You have rituals you do every day like maybe brewing your morning coffee, those you might do once a week like taking the family out for dinner or those that happen less frequently during holidays. Religion is built around rituals and ceremonies.

Rituals provide order and structure to our lives. They also give us that sense of community with those that share our rituals.

If there's any doubt as to the power of rituals, look no farther than the ritual of lining up to be first to the premiere of a new Star Wars movie. People will wait in line for hours, even days, dressed up as their favorite character and they have fun doing it.

Using rituals on YouTube typically come in the form of a welcome message, what you call your community or frequent gestures you make.

For example, one of my favorite YouTubers calls her community bosses and regularly asks them to comment with the word "Boss" to show their agreement with an idea.

I make it a point at the beginning of every video to thank my subscribers for taking a part of their day to join me.

Keep these three ideas in mind when thinking about the rituals you want to use in your videos:

- The ritual should be specific to your audience to really build that sense of community. It's like a secret language that only they know.
- Your ritual should be consistent, something you do in nearly every video or that your community can do regularly.
- The ritual should be easy. Oreo cookies never would have gotten away with a nine-step process for the cookies rather than simply twist, lick, dunk and repeat.

Creating Community through a Common Enemy

Creating a common enemy could be one of the most effective but also the most difficult parts of building your brand.

Nothing binds a community like the acknowledgement that there is a greater power out there, out to get each individual and the only way to beat that enemy is to stick together. We're not just talking about emotions like fear and self-preservation here but also positive ones like courage and a duty to protect those you love.

To be clear, I'm not talking about pitting your community against a specific person or a group of people. There are too many examples from history of tyrants using a common enemy as a scape goat to lead nations to hatred and war. Lately it seems both political parties have taken the idea of a common enemy to dangerous extremes.

Your community's common enemy will likely be more ideological.

For companies in the personal finance space, the common enemy is the lenders, loan sharks, and other power-players that keep people 'poor'. The 'Haves' versus the 'Have-nots'. The 99% versus the 1%.

Other examples of common enemies might include:

- People keeping you from being as successful as possible
- People that want you to be as miserable as they are
- People that hurt other people or animals

Developing the common enemy of your community starts with brainstorming their deepest fears, real or perceived. What are the major hurdles keeping your community from being successful and happy? You can then develop a personification of those fears into an enemy to rally against.

Building Your Brand Around a Leader

Great brands are built around a leader, somebody that represents the entirety of the shared beliefs and what people in the community want to be.

Understand, you are not your community's leader. You're too humble for that. The leader is someone you aspire to be just like the rest of the community. By associating yourself and your brand with the symbolic leader, those beliefs and values embodied by the leader are coupled to your brand.

A couple of points in deciding whom to adopt as your symbolic leader:

- It's best if the person is already deceased. This minimizes the risk some information will come out to tarnish their name or reputation.
- The beliefs and values people attribute to that person should align with those you're trying to develop for your brand.
- Don't be afraid to pick a leader that isn't universally loved. You might be limiting your community a little but this kind of exclusivity will bind the group even closer.

A Few Notes on Branding

Just a few more points to developing your brand and building a community around your business or YouTube channel.

Don't feel like you have to use every brand element in every video.

There will be visual cues to parts of your brand you can get in each video but it would be silly to think you could repeat your creation story every time. Most of the time, you might only reference one or two elements of brand building.

This is fine. You're not trying to turn every single person that views a video into part of your community. Over time and as people see more of your videos, they'll see more of these brand elements and associate themselves closer to your company.

Again, don't be afraid to let your brand evolve or even change abruptly. It's not easy to build a recognizable brand or a strong community so it's not something you want to change often but every brand changes a little over the years.

Be authentic in the beliefs and other elements you use to represent your brand. Trying to pull one over on people and be someone you're not will either come across as sleazy or will eventually unravel as your true nature comes out. Ultimately, your brand and community are about building trust. You can use that trust to grow your business but never betray it.

Building a brand, whether it's on YouTube or for any business, requires a lot of thought and effort but cannot be neglected. Even more important than a traditional business, YouTube channels need to build a community that will support them with time, comments and sharing. This means actively creating your brand and nurturing what people think of when they watch your videos.

Action Steps:
- Watch a few videos from five channels similar to yours. Work through the list of brand elements to see if you can find any and what these channels are branding around.
- What are your most strongly-held beliefs? Which of these do you want to use as your shared beliefs for the community?
- Outline a few moments in your life that developed these beliefs, the big emotional milestones that have shaped your personality.
- Brainstorm a few iconic leaders you might use to represent your brand. If they have public speeches available, look for themes within their speeches that demonstrate their own brand elements.

YOUTUBE VIDEO STRUCTURE [THE HIDDEN SECRET OF CHANNEL SUCCESS]

YouTube video structure could be one of the biggest secrets to getting your channel started and getting the attention you need to grow

Make enough YouTube videos and most people will settle into a structure. People are hard-wired for repetition. Even if you don't consciously try to structure out your videos with some of the ideas we talk about here, you'll subconsciously include them in a routine.

That's how most YouTube creators stumble into a video structure. They never even think about creating a formal plan for structure. It's all that subconscious routine.

And we all know that 'subconsciously' isn't the way to grow your YouTube channel.

You don't just stumble into YouTube growth and you don't go viral by just lucking into the best practices. You have to consciously work at making your videos better.

Making that conscious effort to structure your videos is part of that work.

What is video structure and why is it so important?

Video structure is really two ideas that you incorporate into all of your videos.

First, it's the flow and layout you use in each video. This means the main structural elements like a hook, a channel callout, the video's topic content and some kind of a closing call-to-action.

Adopting some kind of a formal structure like this helps create videos in the least amount of time possible. By starting with that basic outline, you already know what you want to include in each piece and sometimes can even drop in a templated piece of content.

For example, I say the same three sentences after my channel trailer in every video.

"Joseph Hogue with the Let's Talk Money channel here on YouTube. I want to send a special shout-out to everyone in the subscriber community, thank you for taking a part of your day to be here. If you're not part of that community yet, just click that little red subscribe button. It's free and you'll never miss an episode."

We'll talk about some of the branding pieces later in the book but it also makes for an easy way to start my videos, after the hook, before I start in on the content.

Making a conscious format on structure gives your videos organization and flow. One piece naturally leads into the next and it just makes for a better story.

The second idea here, and this is the more important, is that structuring your videos helps make sure you get in as many opportunities to increase engagement and keep people watching. This isn't done just through the formal structure but in the individual pieces you make sure to include in each video.

Do I really need to convince you on the importance of all this?

Wouldn't it be nice to cut half an hour or more from the time it takes to create a video? Wouldn't it be nice to just know, "Okay, this is what I need in this section," instead of struggling with writer's block?

And we know the importance of keeping people watching a video and engaging. Besides number of views, the average view duration of a video is the most important factor in your YouTube success. Those two measures fit together for your total watch-time on a video and determine how aggressively YouTube ranks and promotes it.

Four Main Parts to a YouTube Video Structure

Let's look at that first idea in a YouTube video structure, the formal layout, first and then build in some individual points to drive engagement and community.

If you haven't already gotten the message, I'm going for the broken record award and just want to say this a few more million times... this is the structure I use and the one I've seen used by many other channels, but it's by no means the only way to do it.

Start with this basic structure and add in your own ideas. Experimenting and growing with novel ideas is the way you grow long-term on YouTube.

My videos always include four key elements; the hook, a channel welcome, the content and an end screen call-to-action.

YouTube Video Hook

This is something I picked up from Sunny Lenarduzzi and is a great way to build excitement for your videos.

The hook is a 15- to 45-second intro to your video that tells people what you're going to talk about and why it's important. Many of the larger, professional channels use a hook but Sunny is particularly good at describing how to set it up.

Every hook includes a Hook (yeah, sorry for the double-use), an Outcome and a Testimonial or the HOT acronym.

The hook-piece is one sentence that grabs your audience. It's the very first sentence and designed to shock, amaze, perplex or just excite your viewer. This could be something like a statistic, a question or just an interesting statement.

"The average American eats eight spiders a year while sleeping!"

The outcome statement is a sentence or two and promises exactly what the viewer will get in the video. This is important because you're setting people up to watch the entire video. The hook got them excited. Now they know exactly what they're going to get out of it and will stick around until they get it.

"By the end of this video, I'm going to reveal three ways to stop those eight-legged freaks from crawling into your mouth while you sleep. I'll also show you why that might not be a good thing."

The testimonial helps to build credibility for the outcome. It's the reason people need to watch YOUR video instead of just clicking out to one of the suggested videos on the same topic. It can be proof from someone else or your own experience.

"In fact, I used this process and haven't seen a spider in the house for three years."

(OK, so the example here is a little far-fetched but you get the idea)

There are a lot of people that just start their videos off going right into the content and some will tell you that YouTube viewers just want the goods without all the intro and calls-to-action. That might be true for some viewers but it's no way to grow a channel.

To really grow your channel, add subscribers and get people engaged, you need to get them excited and interested in your video. That means doing more than just delivering some quick content.

Why Use a Channel Welcome in Your Videos

The channel welcome is an easy way to build that sense of community and includes some deep branding ideas that helped me grow from zero to 35,000 subscribers in my first year on YouTube.

- I get to repeat my channel name. People are just starting to see YouTube as a regular source of entertainment and individual channels rather than simply a place to watch funny cat videos. You want to put your channel name in their heads just as the major networks like Fox, ABC and TNT do on television.

- I get to show my appreciation for subs and their time. How much free time do you have in a day? It's a big deal for someone to take 10- or 15-minutes to watch your video. Appreciate that and make sure your viewers know you do.

- I get to build a sense of exclusivity in community. I'm specifically thanking my community and telling people how they can be part of that community by subscribing.

- I lower the mental-cost of subscribing. Being YouTubers, it can be easy to forget that some people don't know that you can subscribe to channels or that it costs nothing. Most people are still casual users of the platform. You want to plant every seed possible to get them to make a commitment to your channel.

You don't need to stretch your channel welcome out beyond two or three sentences. Get those elements in quickly and get on with the content.

Structuring your Video's Content

Just as your overall video has a formal structure to organize it and give it a flow, the content section of your video should have its own structure.

- Lead in with a problem or something to build excitement about the content
- Relate the problem to your solution
- Describe your solution
- Prove how the solution works or will help transform the viewer through a personal story or anecdote
- Summarize what you talked about and why it's important

You don't necessarily have to script out your entire video. I do and will talk about why in a coming chapter, but just outlining your ideas in this structure will help keep you from rambling and will give your content a flow that makes sense.

Wrapping up Your Video with a Call-to-Action

A call-to-action (CTA) is what you want viewers to do whether it be watching another video, subscribing or clicking through to your blog or affiliate.

You can have multiple CTAs throughout your video. Some might call on the viewer to watch for a link in the video description to another video or to a special offer. Some might be to subscribe like in your channel welcome section.

You should limit your CTAs though and repeat your most important towards the end of the video. Pushing too many calls-to-action and your viewer can get overloaded, meaning none of the CTAs really stand out as important and none get clicked.

Putting your most important CTAs towards the end works on a couple of levels. If someone has watched your entire video, they probably liked it or at least were entertained. This increases the likelihood they'll listen to you when you ask them to do something else. Putting a CTA towards the end also means it's one of the last the viewer will hear and will be top-of-mind.

Potential CTAs to include throughout and towards the end of your videos include:

- Subscribing to the channel (don't forget to tell them why they need to subscribe)
- Clicking through to a specific video that goes into detail on a related topic
- Calling out a link to a free lead magnet that will put them on your email list
- Calling out a link to an affiliate offer
- Share their thoughts through a comment
- Support the channel with a 'Like' or sharing the video
- Join you on other social media platforms

How to Structure Your YouTube Videos for Engagement and Community

Even after 200+ videos on YouTube, I still use a checklist for each video. This checklist includes ideas that will help keep people watching, engage them to a CTA or develop that relationship and build community. I don't use every one of these ideas in every video but try to include as many in each video as possible.

- Ask viewers to comment on a specific question. Most people don't think about commenting and won't know what to say unless you ask a specific question that relates to the topic.
- Include and tease 'bonus' content that comes at the end of the video. This can be an extra idea or quick-win trick or anything that adds to the topic. This helps keep people watching even if the main content loses their interest.
- Refer to other videos. Keeping people on your channel or even just on YouTube after your video is a huge signal to YouTube and one of the biggest factors in boosting views. If you have a video that goes further into a topic, refer to it and include a card or link in the video description.
- Use graphic interrupts! This can be anything from text on

the screen to showing an image or screenshare clip. It's anything that breaks up the monotony of watching your pretty face for 15 minutes and it's critical to boosting your average view duration. These can include informational graphics and charts, funny images or just b-roll. I usually try having some kind of graphic or text interrupt every minute but sometimes even every 30 seconds.

- Humor...even if it's bad jokes! It can be tough for educational channels, especially in themes like personal finance, to get humor across. Remember though, education isn't enough when people have hundreds of thousands of other channels competing for their time. Fit elements into each video that entertain, amuse or surprise viewers.

- Use a personal story or testimonial. People learn from education but they're engaged by stories. Even a list-video about making a casserole can draw people in with that tragic casserole experience you had or the story you heard.

- Brand Building – we talked about the different ways to build your brand on YouTube in a previous chapter but it's important to make a note to include these ideas in each video. Your brand is one of the only things that separates you from all the other channels on YouTube and the only reason why someone would subscribe. You won't include every element of brand-building in every video but you always need to be thinking about how to include a few.

- 'Talk up' what you're currently covering or about to cover every minute or so. Attention spans are notoriously low on YouTube. Keep people interested by every-so-often talking about how important an idea is or teasing what you're going to reveal next within the video.

- No summary language towards the end of the video. While it's good to summarize or repeat some ideas towards the end of a video, don't let viewers know that's what you're doing. Using phrases like, "In summary," or "To wrap it up," just tells people that the video is over and they should start looking for other videos in the suggested column. Be providing valuable information or entertainment all the way to your final call-to-action and end screen

It might be a lot to consider for every video you produce but trying to hit as many of these points as possible will really boost your channel watch-time, engagement and lead to more subscribers. You probably won't fit every element in every video, unless you're a superstar, but make a conscious effort to check through the list each time.

I realize this seems like a very formulaic way of setting up your videos and it can be tempting to just go in and talk conversationally through instead. If you can just talk through a video, hitting every element above every time, you're an exceptional person. For the rest of us, at least outlining your video with this formal structure will help make sure all your videos are as entertaining and engaging as possible. That's going to translate to longer watch-time, more subscribers and a channel that grows fast!

Action Steps:

- Create a document template you can use for each video including the formal structure you want to include; i.e. intro, channel welcome, content and final CTA.

- Copy down some of the individual elements like a comment CTA or request for people to 'Like' your video. Add some of your own ideas to the list and check back on the list while developing each video.

HOW TO SHOOT A VIDEO FOR YOUTUBE

Just a few basics can have you recording a video for YouTube within an hour with all the professional-quality you see on the biggest channels

There are so many ways to record a video for YouTube, it's almost like having too many choices. From just pressing record on your smartphone to setting up a studio in your home, creators have more options than they can handle.

I know a lot of creators that spend hours a week, sometimes hours a day, watching channels on photography and cinematography. They spend more time learning video tricks than they do creating content.

That's not to say there aren't some cool things you can do with your camera, but it should never be at the expense of your content. Stick with the basics of recording a video and spend the rest of your time on content and building your channel.

In this chapter, I'm going to focus on that home studio setup with the basics and some advanced tips for making your videos look as professional as possible.

Ways to Record a Video for YouTube

Let's back up for one second though and talk about the different ways to record a video for YouTube. While you might use one of these methods for most of your videos, it's important to know all the options and possibly to throw each in the mix from time-to-time.

Giving your community a little variety in your video style is a great way to keep things fresh. Some of the video styles are more personal while others look more professional. Pulling from each of these styles occasionally will help keep your community interested and keep your videos from feeling stale.

- DSLR or video camera, studio set-up – means professional

lighting, high-quality video and audio and really makes your videos look polished.

- Webcam recording is more personal but can also look less professional or edited. Great for screenshares and walk-through demonstrations.
- Vlog-style with a smartphone is the height of that personal-feel but you'll need to make sure you don't sacrifice audio or video quality in the process.

While we'll spend the rest of the chapter talking about how to set up a studio shoot for your videos, I want to reinforce the idea that you should be using all three of these methods. Use your webcam for informal live streams or other events and reach out with a vlog-style video every once in a while.

How to Set Up Your Equipment for YouTube Videos

I can't teach you how to be a professional videographer. First because I don't consider myself a master videographer, though I get paid for creating videos. Second because the book would be three-times as long.

The great part about YouTube is, you don't need to be an expert in photography or video. The platform is naturally a more informal, less produced media. People don't expect your videos to have all the editing and production they see on a TV drama series.

That doesn't mean you can just flip on your camera and start recording but it does mean that a few tips and basics will take you as far as you need to go.

That's what I want to do here. Guide you through the basics and the tips I've picked up recording for YouTube.

Lighting
- The standard three-point lighting is easy to set up and control shadows. You'll have two lights in front, a 'key light' and a 'fill light'. Then you'll have a 'back light' shining down to illuminate your head and shoulders. Generally, the key light is a little brighter than the fill light and the backlight will usually be the weakest of the three.

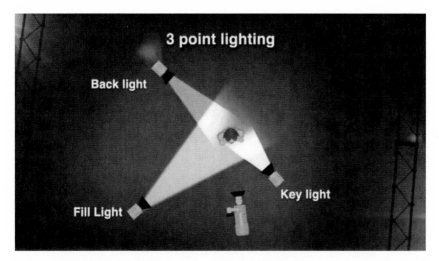

3 point lighting

Back light

Fill Light

Key light

- This setup really makes you stand out from the background, something you don't see in a lot of informal YouTube videos. You can substitute a single ring-light in front if you like but don't skimp on the hair light in back.

- Check your background for reflective surfaces and check the video display for reflections of lighting or equipment. Adjust your lights higher or lower, or move things in the background to remove reflections.

- Check on your video display that your lighting is even, i.e. no shadows on either side of your face.

- Make sure your lighting equipment isn't showing in the video.

Other Equipment Setup and Notes

- Try to hide the lav mic behind your shirt or just out of frame if possible. You can also use a boom mic to keep it out of the video.

- Have extra batteries and battery packs for your camera and other equipment standing by. Make it a routine to recharge all batteries the day before your weekly shoot.

- Check the white balance on your camera. Most DSLR cameras will have an automatic white balance that works well but you can get a little better color by setting it yourself.

- Check to make sure your backdrop is framed right and all shelves or pictures are level.

- Mark a spot on the floor to which you can return for each take. This will make editing and continuity much easier.
- If you're using a teleprompter, practice reading from it just before recording to make sure the scroll speed and other features are set right.

Getting ready to record, make sure you have at least twice the time available as the length of the finished video. For example, if you're script is 3,000 words and you read at an average pace of 180 words per minute, then the finished video should be somewhere around 16 minutes long. That means you want to have at least 32 minutes free for recording to get all the way through.

As a beginner, you'll make more mistakes and will probably need closer to three-times the video length to record. Of course, this is if you're going for a fairly mistake-free video where you stop and re-record clips each time you make a mistake. If you're just speaking impromptu from notes and are not worried about the ums and other gaffes, you might be able to run through your video more quickly.

Make sure you turn off all fans, air conditioning and anything else that could be picked up by the microphone. Good audio is critical to a video, maybe even more important than the video quality.

Finally, before shooting your video, read through the script one more time to remind yourself with where you want to add emphasis and pauses.

Recording a Video for YouTube

Once you have all your equipment set up, actually recording your video is the easy part. You'll tap the record button on your camera and your digital recorder, then just start talking.

There are a few more notes though to make your recording go as smoothly as possible.

- Some older DSLR cameras limit video recording to 12-minute segments on file size. Make a habit of being aware how long your video is going so your camera doesn't stop recording without you knowing it. I recommend shooting for no more than about 10-minute clips so you build that habit of knowing when to restart your camera.

- Make it a point to check that your camera and digital audio recorder are both recording before you start a new clip.

- If you're going for a mistake-free video, understand you might have to do several takes of a section. Relax and just try to read naturally from the prompter. Play around with the scroll and other settings to make your reading as natural as possible.

- Try to stay in the right frame of mind for the material. For most videos, this will mean smiling and an excited tone. Your enthusiasm and emotion will come through on the video.

Recording videos for YouTube doesn't have to be complicated and you don't need to be an expert in photography. Get the basics down and don't worry about spending too much time mastering all the tricks of cinematography. Learn how to use your camera to shoot a clear video and how to use your lighting and audio equipment to make a quality production. Spend that time you saved by sticking with the basics of recording to focus more on your video content and you'll never regret it.

Action Steps:

- Practice delivering a speech or topic in front of the camera from notes before you buy a teleprompter. If you find yourself missing parts or making more mistakes than you like, consider buying a prompter and working from that.

- Practice a few video ideas in each of the three formats; presentation style, webcam with a screenshare and vlog style. This will familiarize you with the three video formats and you can pick which you prefer to do most often.

- Set up your equipment and record a video. Then upload it as unlisted to YouTube to see how it turns out. Compare the video and audio quality with other channels.

EASY EDITING TRICKS AND TIPS

Editing videos for YouTube can be frustrating but just a few tips will make any creator look like a professional

Editing your videos can be one of the most time-consuming parts for new YouTube channels but there's also a lot of opportunity in the process. Not only will good editing make even the most awkward, camera-shy person look good but it can help keep people watching your videos longer.

On the upside to the difficulty most beginners run into with editing their own videos, you know this is a natural barrier to entry for competition. Unlike blogging or even podcasting, the additional work it takes to film and edit video help to limit your competition on YouTube.

It will take some time to get proficient in editing your videos. Those first dozen or so videos are going to take longer and you'll be tempted to throw in the towel. Don't give up! Once you get a process, a routine down for editing your videos, it's going to feel natural and you'll be able to do it in less time.

Learning to Edit YouTube Videos

This chapter isn't meant to teach you everything you need to know about editing or working with your editing software. Every editing software comes with tutorials to get you started quickly with the basics. What I want to do here is take you beyond those basics with some hints and tricks I've picked up on that will make your videos look more professional.

I'll be using the Camtasia video editing product for the chapter and screenshots but the features I'll be pointing out are available on any editing software.

A note on choosing editing software is appropriate here. There are free packages you can use like Blender and OpenShot but most fall short on the features and tutorials you need to make quality videos. Most will upsell you into their premium features anyway so you might as well start from the standpoint of finding the best premium editing software.

I use Camtasia but have also tested Adobe Premiere Pro and Final Cut Pro. Each has its pros and cons but are all three great products and which you choose will largely be a matter of taste.

Editing Your YouTube Videos

You'll first need to upload all your video and audio files into the editor. Note that your editing software might not accept all file types so you might have to convert the video files.

For example, Camtasia doesn't work with .mov files which (of course) is the file created by my Canon Rebel. To use the files, I have to convert them using the free Handbrake software into an mp4 file then upload to Camtasia.

You'll also need to upload all your graphics and backgrounds you plan on using in the video. This is where that pre-production process of scripting and using production notes really comes in handy. It is so much easier, and time-friendly, to decide where you want to place graphics and text in your videos while scripting instead of trying to do this during editing.

Any graphics or backgrounds you use regularly like a subscribe graphic or end screen, you'll want to put in a library on the editing software. This will save you from having to upload the graphic every time you make a new video.

Tutorials for your video editor will get you started with the basics of placing clips on the timeline and making cuts. What I want to do for the rest of the chapter is to walk through some tricks I use in editing and some of my favorite features.

I'll also be walking through these features and how to use the editing software in our accompanying video course to the book. **Click to see all the videos in the course.**

One of the most important parts of the process is splicing clips together so you get a continuous flow to the video. Few video creators can get through their entire video or script without making at least a few mistakes and cuts.

Having a start point on the floor where you end and begin each clip will help but you'll never line these up perfectly. Simply splicing the two clips together will get a 'jump' in the video where your body position will be different from one second to the next.

Fixing this means creating a 'jump cut' in the video. Look closely and you'll notice this in any recorded video from commercials to movies and TV. It's where a person continues speaking through two clips but the camera angle or video zoom changes. It might look like this is done for emphasis on what the person is saying or cinematography but it's really done to splice those two clips together.

Some creative ways to splice clips together for jump cuts:

- The most common method, and easiest, is just to zoom in the second clip 10% to 20%. Cut the second clip right to the beginning of the first word, I usually cut it right to the point where my mouth is starting to move on the words. Then you can increase the video image size to that clip so that you are a longer portion of the screen. The result is that the video jumps from your first clip into the second with a quick close-up.

- Another great jump cut trick is using a second camera, set at a 45-degree angle, while filming. Instead of doing the close-up jump cut for splicing two clips, you can use a clip from the second camera for that section of video. It takes more work managing the two video files but it's a very professional look.

- When in doubt, you can also add extra graphics to cover up clip splicing. Add a quick plain background with notes for a definition or some b-roll.

There are some features in editing software that you'll want to take advantage of to make your videos look professional and engaging.

- Lower Thirds – are graphics that appear in the lower-third of your screen and show names/titles of people in the video. You'll notice these in newscasts and they're easy to use.

- Text Annotations are a simple way to get text on the screen to keep the viewer's focus on the video. You can put it overlapping your video or cut to a flat background you use for definitions and bullet points.

- Arrows and Circle animations are easy ways to draw attention to one part of the screen and make your videos more dynamic.

- Reveal behaviors on text is a special way of having your text appear which gives it a 'typewriter' effect as if you are typing on the screen.

- Animations to zoom-in or pan out on an image are an easy way to use image b-roll but make it look more dynamic like a video.

Once you're done editing the video, make sure you download it and watch it all the way through. You've put so much time into this production, don't publish a video with bad editing errors for lack of reviewing your finished video.

Once you're happy with how the edited video looks, you have several options for uploading. Most editing software will integrate and allow you to upload directly to YouTube. I like to download an mp4 file as a backup and then upload that to YouTube.

This was by no means a complete video editing tutorial. You'll need to watch through the basics tutorials for whichever video editing software you choose but the tips shared in this chapter will help you go beyond the basics to a more professional-looking video. It's the little details, the extra graphics and animations that will help your videos stand out on YouTube.

THE RIGHT WAY TO UPLOAD A VIDEO TO YOUTUBE FOR MASSIVE VIEWS

Don't miss an opportunity to boost your YouTube video before it even goes live with these tips on uploading

Uploading a video to YouTube is deceptively simple but the basic process misses out on some of the most effective ways of making your channel a success.

Besides the ability to 'tell' the world's second-largest search engine what your video is about, the upload process is your opportunity to hook viewers and get them to do exactly what you want.

The upload process is part of that professional side of managing a YouTube channel, the part that isn't immediately clear until you put in the time to really understand how the business works.

Spending your time here, researching and understanding how to use the process effectively, will be that extra push you need to see fast channel growth.

Let's look at the basics of uploading a video to YouTube before getting into the details that matter.

How to Upload a Video to YouTube

Spend any time watching cat videos on YouTube and you'll realize that uploading a video is (almost) too easy.

Click the plus icon in upper-right menu to upload a video. You'll have the option to upload as public, unlisted, private or scheduled.

- Uploading a video as public will publish it immediately
- Unlisted videos are only available to viewers with the URL link
- Private videos are only available to viewers you invite to watch, with a maximum of 50 invites
- Scheduled videos become public on the scheduled day and time

Once you choose how to upload your video, you'll see the main video creation page below. There are four important parts here plus the scheduling section we'll detail in the chapter.

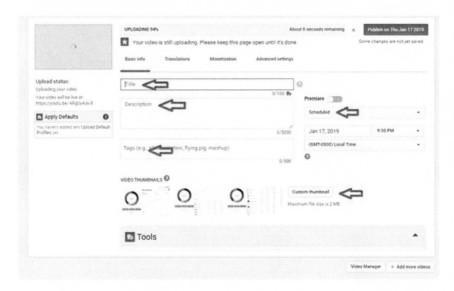

YouTube accepts most of the common video formats including mp4, mov, avi, wmv and FLV. If you get an error message uploading, try using free conversion software like Handbrake to convert into mp4.

Longer video files can take a while to upload and process. A 15-minute mp4 file will take over half an hour to upload. You'll need to keep the browser tab open while it's uploading but you can open other internet tabs while you wait.

We'll talk about four main parts of the upload screen [title, description, tags, thumbnails] in separate sections below.

Once your video is uploaded, you'll have the option of adding closed captioning, cards and an end screen.

Adding Closed Captioning to Your Videos is important for a couple of reasons. About one-in-twenty people have issues with hearing loss so adding captions will allow you to serve this community. There are also those that choose to use captioning if they're watching at work or somewhere the sound would be distracting. I generally see about 8% of my viewers using closed captioning.

Closed captions are also another way to tell YouTube what your video is about and help it to rank in search. The platform creates its own set of captions but seems to not trust these enough to use for search discovery.

If you script out your videos and use a teleprompter, captioning is easy because you can just copy-paste your text into the captions box.

- On the video information screen, click to Subtitles/CC
- Click to Add New Subtitles and select the language
- Choose Transcribe and auto-sync
- Paste your text in the box or type your captions
- It will take an hour or more for YouTube to sync up the text and audio, then click back through and approve the captions

You can also hire a service like Rev.com to transcribe your videos. The service charges a dollar per minute which can add up for new creators.

We'll talk about scripting and using a teleprompter throughout the book and this is another one of the benefits. There's a learning curve to making a prompted video look natural, and I'm not sure I've got it down yet, but the pros outweigh the cons. Besides being able to easily add captions to a video, scripting out my videos and reading from the prompter cuts editing time in half.

Adding Cards to Your Video takes less than two minutes and will help to keep people watching your channel.

Cards are the notifications you see appear in the upper-right of the video, prompting a viewer to watch another video or do something else. There are five types of cards you can add:

- Promote another video or playlist. I like to prompt playlists instead of individual videos because they lead to longer watch-time.
- Promote another channel. This can be helpful if you're doing a collab with another creator.
- Feature a non-profit for a donation.
- Ask viewers to participate in a poll. I'll have to admit, I rarely

see this one used though it sounds like an excellent way to get info on your viewers and increase engagement.

- Link to an approved website. This includes your associated website, a merchandise site or a crowdfunding platform.

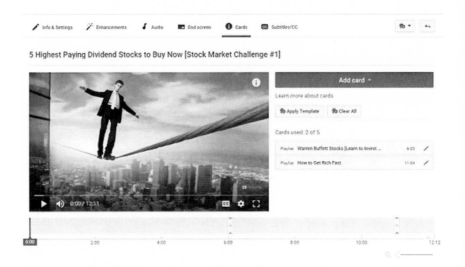

I recommend adding at least two cards in each video. I add my first card right around the 50% point of the length, the average duration for most of my videos. The idea is that it keeps people watching distraction-free for as long as possible but gives them something to click when their attention starts dropping.

Adding End Screens to Your YouTube videos is another easy process and another way to keep people on your channel.

An end screen is the last 10 – 20 seconds of video where you can prompt viewers to watch specific videos next or include your subscribe call-to-action. YouTube makes this easy by showing end screen elements at fixed points on the screen.

The easiest way to add an end screen is to use one of the templates provided by YouTube by clicking Use Template. You'll be shown a selection of formats with video boxes or a subscribe prompt at different points on the screen.

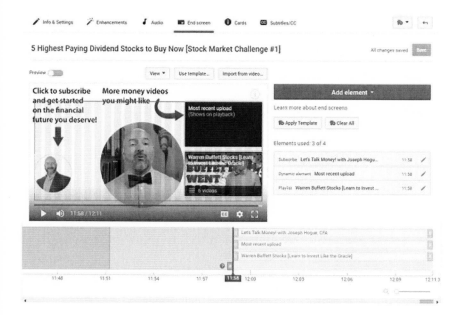

If you know which template you'll be using, you can edit your video to include text callouts pointing to the elements. For example, just above the Subscribe element on my end screen template, I ask people to click with an arrow pointing to the image.

You're given a choice of prompting viewers to watch your most recent upload, a selected video or playlist, or allowing YouTube to pick the video most appropriate to a viewer's history.

- I always select Most Recent Upload for the first video element shown. This helps to send as much traffic as possible to your newest video to give it that critical watch-time push during those first two days.

- I used to trust that YouTube knew my viewers better than I and would select Best for Viewer for the second video element. Instead, I've switched to adding a playlist here because they usually translate into greater watch-time per viewer.

It's important to be talking and providing content through your end screen. Ending the informational part of the video tells viewers there's nothing left and they'll be easily distracted by suggested videos and other content. Instead, keep them focused on your video while you prompt them to click through on the end screen itself.

You can adjust the timing of your end screen elements up to 20 seconds of your video.

Scheduling Your YouTube Videos

I've talked to creators that have hundreds of thousands of subscribers that are still publishing their videos immediately after uploading. They might have a specific day and time they like to publish each week but they wait until the last minute to get their videos done.

That just sounds exhausting to me and one unexpected delay can cause them to disappoint their community.

I know it's tough getting videos done weeks in advance but once you're scheduled ahead, it takes no extra effort to stay out ahead. As long as you keep producing the same number of videos each week that you publish, you'll always be scheduled in advance and will never have to worry about not being ready with a video.

Think about it this way, if Seinfeld didn't have an episode ready for Must See Thursday...how happy do you think NBC would be?

A professional channel means having a video ready for the same day and time each week, optimally for several days per week. The only way you can do this reliably is to work at least a couple of weeks in advance and schedule your videos.

Uploading a video to YouTube will become routine quickly. The basic process is so simple that it can be easy to mindlessly zoom through it.

Resist that temptation!

Put just as much time into researching the metadata and points below as you do producing your videos. Do it for every single video and you'll see growth like you wouldn't believe!

Video Metadata for YouTube Success

While some of the parts of uploading like the description and tags are evident in the process, their importance isn't nearly as obvious and the basic upload process misses a huge chance to take your videos farther.

This opportunity is centered around something called metadata… sorry, couldn't resist a nerd word.

Metadata is just data (information) that describes other data. In this case, metadata is things that describe what your video is about.

That's important because YouTube isn't a person. The platform can't watch your video and say, "OK, this video is about paying off debt. I'll rank it with these videos about debt." While YouTube and its parent-company Google are masters at understanding content, it still needs help at times and it never hurts to nudge it in the direction you want.

In fact, there's evidence that metadata on a video (especially the tags, title and description) are even more important during the first week. It's in this period that YouTube doesn't have a lot of its own data on how viewers react to the video so it uses your metadata to help rank it quickly in the relevant topics.

We covered some of this metadata information in the chapter on Finding Video Ideas for YouTube. This metadata information like keywords (tags) and title are so important that you need to do this research before scripting and producing the video.

Knowing what keywords you'll be targeting in your video before you produce it will help create something that sounds natural instead of stuffed with unrelated concepts.

An important note about metadata for your YouTube videos. Think long and hard about changing the metadata to a video after it's been published and NEVER change the metadata on a video that is performing well.

When your video is published, YouTube begins to measure how well it performs on views and watch-time for the keywords used. This is how your video ranks for search and suggested videos on YouTube. If you change the metadata, it resets everything and YouTube must relearn how appropriate the metadata is for the video.

That's not to say you should never change metadata after a video is published. If it's been more than six months and the video is doing nothing then refocusing the keywords and rewriting the description might give it new life.

How to Pick Your YouTube Video Tags

Any old school blogger remembers the days you could just stuff an article with a keyword to rank on Google. Bloggers would even group keywords in a list in a jumbled paragraph of words to rank.

It started that way on YouTube as well, where you could just stuff your keywords into the description and tag field to rank...ah the glory days of easy traffic.

Sadly [or fortunately, depending on how you look at it] that's no longer the case. The tag field on your video upload isn't as important as it once was but the research you'll do to find the best tags is still extremely important.

A new channel cannot hope to rank for the most competitive keywords. You can tag and use the keywords in your description all you want but you probably aren't showing up anywhere near the top 20 for a keyword like 'making money online'.

Instead, you go further out into niche ideas like 'making money as a teenager'. Better to rank a video in the top five for a lower-traffic keyword than buried in the 50th position for a high-traffic one.

So your keyword research can start with a core topic, a popular idea and based on a high-traffic keyword, but then you branch out into niche ideas around that topic. This is going to uncover smaller keywords you can use in your description and tag fields. You can also develop a content strategy around this, producing individual videos around each keyword in the group.

- Smaller channels, under 25K subscribers, should aim for keywords that get between 100 to 1,000 monthly searches on YouTube. Remember, you can use the Keywords Everywhere Chrome extension to see monthly traffic.
- Start typing your core topic idea in search to see what is auto-populated by YouTube for niche ideas
- Use the alphabet-search method where you type your core topic keyword in search and then run through the alphabet,

adding each letter to the end of your keyword to see what ideas auto-populate

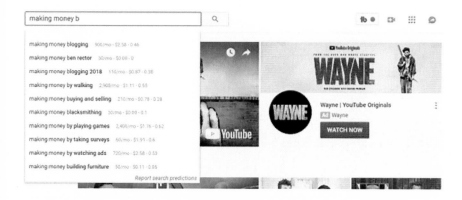

Ideally, you want between 10 and 15 niche keywords related to your video. You'll use these in your tag field and in the video description. One of these, the most relevant, will be your main keyword that you'll target and will go in your title as well.

You can use up to 500 characters in your tag field, which can be a lot of keyword phrases. I don't think you need to use all this space but try using at least 10 or so tags. These keyword phrases of three or four words need to all be related and relevant to your video so they help YouTube understand what it's about.

Creating a Viral Video Title

I hate thumbnails and titles! I hate the idea that you can't just create an excellent video and expect to get views. You also must create an engaging title and a persuasive thumbnail or nobody will click through to see your amazing video.

Frustrating but that's just how it is. Put in the time for each title and thumbnail and it'll be time well spent.

Creating a great title is one-part art and two parts work. That's a good thing for those of us that don't consider themselves artistically-gifted because it means you don't have to be Ernest Hemingway to create a great title, you just have to put in the work.

Let's start with a few points and then I'll share a free tool that can help with the process.

- Your title should include your main keyword or phrase. This is no longer as important in Google search but is still very much so in YouTube search and evidence shows titles with the keyword first do better than having it towards the end.

- Three types of titles do better than any others; lists, how-to and questions.

- Character length needs to be shorter, around 70 characters, but data shows that titles between 50 – 60 characters tend to perform best.

- You can include [ ] brackets to separate one part of the title from another part, for example "7 Passive Income Ideas [Proven $5K a Month]"

- Use words that spark emotions like fear, anxiety, happiness. For example, words like blissful, terrifying or surprise.

- Use words that spark curiosity like "you won't believe" or "you'll be amazed"

Creating your best title isn't about inspiration, it's about brainstorming. It's about spending at least 15 minutes writing out different ideas, searching on Google to get ideas, and then narrowing it down to the best one.

One tool I like to use for ideas is social tool CoSchedule. They've created a nice headline analyzer that grades your title ideas on a scale from 0 to 100. The tool looks for points like title length, emotion words, power words and other factors.

https://coschedule.com/headline-analyzer

Understand that the headline analyzer isn't a perfect title creator but it's a useful tool to test out different ideas to see what gets a higher score. Use your own intuition as well to pick the title you end up using.

How to Write Your YouTube Video Description

I'm amazed at how little time creators spend on their video description. Even some large channels often put very little into the description besides a jumble of links.

Your video description is a great opportunity on several levels and it's something that absolutely cannot be neglected.

Not only does your description help YouTube understand how and where to rank your videos, it also gives you the chance to make money, keep viewers on your channel longer and convert subscribers.

You're allowed up to 5,000 characters in your video description, around 800 words, but you probably don't need to use all of it. I aim for around 300 words to describe the video and then add a template section with subscribe links and other content which is around 150 words.

Some things to consider including in your description,

- A keyword-rich description of your video (duh). Use keywords from your tag research here and make it persuasive. Talk up what you'll be sharing and why someone should watch the video. Make this at least a couple hundred words long or more.

- Consider adding something like a Table of Contents after your description, write out the time where each main point appears in the video (Example 1:23). This will keep people watching instead of getting bored and clicking out, plus it gives you another chance to include keyword-rich topics.

- Callout relevant videos and add a link to each. This is a great way to keep viewers on your channel, a huge signal to YouTube and one of the best ways to convert subscribers.

- Include a couple of relevant affiliate links. Not too many and only ones directly related to the content.

- Have a one- or two-sentence callout for why someone should subscribe and then add your subscribe link.

- Have a callout to any related link magnets for an email list.

Remember, YouTube is just a machine. It needs the user (YOU) to help it understand what a video is about through the metadata. HELP YouTube HELP You!

The first few lines of your video description will show up in search and are given extra weight by YouTube so make sure you include your most important keyword here as well as something persuasive to get viewers to click through.

A note about links that take people off YouTube. Like any social platform, YouTube doesn't like when you send people away from the site. Viewers clicking off YouTube from your videos can hurt your search ranking while viewers staying on the platform after your vids help it.

That doesn't mean you should never add a link that points off-YouTube. Making money through affiliate links and adding people to your email list are good reasons but within reason. Affiliate links should be highly-relevant to the video content.

It's up to you what you include in your video description but I've seen some pretty weird stuff you might want to avoid including:

- A long clickable list of video equipment – are your viewers REALLY that interested in it and is the pennies you make on Amazon worth hurting your video by sending them off YouTube?

- Random affiliates that don't relate to the video. YouTube sees an off-site link even if your viewers aren't clicking on it so this might be hurting you more than helping.

- Too many social media links. This one is debatable. You should be trying to build a community on other platforms but make sure you're really using those platforms if you're going to be taking viewers off YouTube.

How to Create a YouTube Video Thumbnail

Thumbnails and titles are extremely frustrating...have I said that yet?

The flip-side to the importance of your thumbnail and title is that, if you get good at creating these, they can draw in more people than you'd imagine. I've heard of creators literally spending hours on a title and thumbnail for each video. That seems like a bit much but any time you spend learning how to create a great thumbnail will be well spent.

Let's look at some thumbnail basics and then I'll share my process.

A profile pic, an image of your face, is a critical part of your thumbnail. New videos will go out to your subscribers in their feed first and it's these first interactions that tell YouTube whether to show the video to more people. Since your subscribers know you, they're more likely to click on your thumbnail if it includes your face.

In fact, I've put other people's images on my thumbnails before [people much more popular and well-known than I] and have seen the videos get lower than normal views. Subscribers may or may not recognize someone else so it's always best to put your image on the thumbnail.

I'll detail an easy way to make profile pics for your thumbs later but they should include expressive emotions like surprise, shock and happiness. Your profile pic should also be fairly large, taking up at least a quarter or a third of the thumbnail. Remember, most people are going to be seeing it on a small screen.

I like to add a few words on the thumbnail though I know creators that do well with no text at all. The idea is to create interest or a question in the mind of a potential viewer. Your thumbnail should tell a story that complements the video title.

For example, in the thumbnail above about warning signs to a dividend cut, I have knives in the background image and use language that evokes fear and uncertainty. I might have been able to do this without the text but I like adding a couple of words on each thumbnail.

If you do decide to add text to your thumbnails, I would strongly recommend adding no more than three to five words. Any more than that and it will be difficult to read on a smartphone and is just going to jumble up your thumbnail.

The recommended thumbnail size for uploading to YouTube is 1280x720 pixels but remember that most people will see yours on a smartphone. While creating your thumbnail, always decrease the size to 100x56 to see how it looks at the smaller size.

Designing your thumbnails, it helps to use a consistent text font and colors. This will help people recognize your videos when they're scrolling quickly and helps to brand your channel.

Finally, the decision to use an image background or flat color background is a tough one. I like using images because it helps to tell a story about the video but they can also be distracting and make it difficult to read the text.

There are a lot of channels that use a flat background or some simple text graphics besides their profile pic for thumbnails. Check out the thumbnails on Nick Nimmin's and Derral Eves' channels for examples. I don't think there is any ONE way to do it. My suggestion is to try it out on a few videos, using images and a flat background, to see which you like and which result in higher click-through.

I know a lot of people like to take a simple screenshot from their video to create a thumbnail. It's a simple solution but I have a process that goes just a little further for a more professional result.

- Take lots of profile pics. This means standing in front of the camera [with the image from chest to head] and snapping pics in different poses and facial expressions.
- You can then use a site like ClippingMagic to cut out the images, creating PNG files you can use to layer your profile image on top of a thumbnail.
- Upload all your profile images to a site like Canva to create your thumbnails
- You can use Canva to create a flat colored background or

grab background images from a site like DepositPhotos and upload to Canva

- Click 'Arrange' in the upper-right on Canva to layer images and text
- Click 'Filter' in the top left on Canva to change images, I like to increase the Saturation for background images to +20 to really bring out the colors
- I use the Alfa Slab One font for text to produce thick lettering that's easy to read
- Copy your text and create another box with the letters in black to place behind but slightly to the left and lower for an outline effect. This really helps separate your text from the background.
- Adding my profile image, I copy-paste another image and increase the Contrast/Brightness to max in the Filter settings. Layering this behind my profile image creates a halo effect.
- In the Filter dropdown, I change the Contrast to +27 and the Blur to -27 on my profile pic. This makes the image really pop-out from the thumbnail.

It takes some experimenting but you'll pick it up quickly and will be able to create your thumbnails within a few minutes once you've got an idea. As with everything here, this isn't the ONLY way to do it but a process I've found that works and results in clickable thumbnails.

* An important note here, changing your thumbnail on a video doesn't change the metadata like changing the title, tags or

description. That means you can change your thumbnail, testing different ideas, without worrying about destroying the momentum for a video.

For thumbnail testing, I usually wait a few weeks and then look to videos getting below-average click-through. This usually means videos with a CTR below 3% for potential thumbnail problems.

I'll record the CTR for the video, create a different thumbnail and replace it on YouTube. After a couple of weeks, I'll look at the new CTR to decide either to keep the new thumb, replace it with another or just go back to the original thumbnail.

Uploading Your YouTube Video to a Playlist

Playlists are another important but often neglected part of your channel. Every time you add a video to a playlist, it creates a new URL that is a signal to YouTube. It's almost like creating new content without having to do anything!

Every video should be in at least one playlist and can be in multiple playlists on your channel or on other creators' channels. In fact, one of the easiest ways to collab with someone is just to add some of their videos to your playlists.

This doesn't mean you have to add a video to a playlist immediately upon upload. I like to wait a week or more to add videos to playlists.

- Create a spreadsheet of video titles and the share link.
- Add a column to note in which playlists the video is included.
- Set a schedule to upload a video to a playlist on days when you don't publish a new video.
- Try keeping playlists to no more than 10 videos and create new playlists as you go

This is the longest chapter by far in the book. That should give you an idea on how important it is to upload a YouTube video using metadata and other concepts to boost your views. These are the kinds of things that the majority of creators don't know about or neglect altogether. Putting in the time to make your video standout will mean the difference between viral success and just another wannabe.

Action Steps:

- Create a checklist or brief outline for uploading a video, using the steps in this chapter. Working through the steps will become second nature after a few dozen videos but you'll need the checklist to make sure you don't miss steps at first.

- Make it a point, each time you upload a video, to search for the main keyword on YouTube. Review some of the titles and thumbnails on ranked videos and click through to check out their descriptions and tags. This will give you ideas when you're uploading your own video.

HOW TO USE YOUTUBE ANALYTICS TO GROW A CHANNEL FAST

Learn how to use data on your YouTube channel to make better videos and get more subscribers

Using analytics to improve your YouTube channel is what truly separates the professionals from the amateurs. It's this point, when you make a commitment to data-driven improvement, that gives your channel the opportunity to grow beyond the millions of hobby channels on the platform.

Fortunately, you don't have to be a numbers nerd like me to understand your video analytics and use it for growth. In fact, YouTube makes it easy to get detailed information about your videos and get ideas.

Let's look at some basic ideas to using your YouTube analytics then I'll show you five points of information that will take you to the next level.

How to Use YouTube Analytics

I hated math and anything to do with statistics in school. It wasn't even until after college that I started seeing the practical use in numbers and how to unlock this 'secret language'. You're going to see a lot of percentages and numbers in this book. Try to remember one thing as you read through and apply the knowledge, numbers don't lie!

The information you get from YouTube about your videos will be an unbiased and straight-forward insight into improving your videos. Don't 'hate' the numbers and don't look for reasons to disbelieve. Trust the numbers and look for ways to improve.

One of the biggest mistakes creators make is getting hung up on comparing their channels to another on the platform. You see the growth in another channel or happen to hear what click-through-rate (CTR) they're getting...and it drives you crazy.

Pretty soon, all you can think about is why your growth is so slow in comparison or what you're doing wrong. You might even start thinking YouTube is being unfair, favoring the other channel over yours.

It's ridiculously frustrating and leads to one thing, creators quitting their channel.

Stop comparing your channel to others! I know it seems impossible to do and in complete transparency, I still can't resist making this kind of comparison myself every so often.

Instead, you need to make a practice of comparing your channel against...your channel. Compare the metrics you see below against where you were at 90 days ago or your analytics over the last year. Doing this forces you to look for that constant improvement, making each video 1% better than the last.

This is the secret to long-term success as a YouTube creator. Make your channel better every video.

One way I like to do this is to create comparison groups in the YouTube Studio analytics. This is a great way to get better comparisons on ways to improve rather than just comparing a single video against another.

Not to get all stats-nerdy on you but you can't rely on a change in one video to prove that it's a better way to do something. Say I wanted to improve my thumbnails for better CTR and decided to use a black background instead of an image background.

If I just made the change in one thumbnail and saw a huge jump in the CTR versus my average in previous videos, does this tell me I should switch to a black background for all videos?

Of course not. It could have been a really great title or some other factor that led to the jump in the CTR. What you need to do, to make sure it's that one change that leads to improvement, is to compare several videos with the change against a group without it.

Doing that means creating two video or playlist groups in your analytics, one group of videos with the change and the other without. Then you can compare metrics like retention, CTR and other analytics between the two groups.

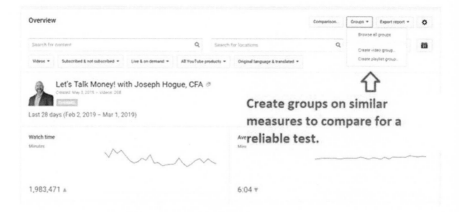

Create groups on similar measures to compare for a reliable test.

Following YouTube Video Retention

Improving your video retention is a great place to start when looking at your analytics. Along with the number of views you get on a video, how long you keep them watching is the biggest factor in your total watch-time. That makes retention and CTR the two most important measures you can watch.

To find your audience retention, go to Audience Retention in your analytics and click on an individual video.

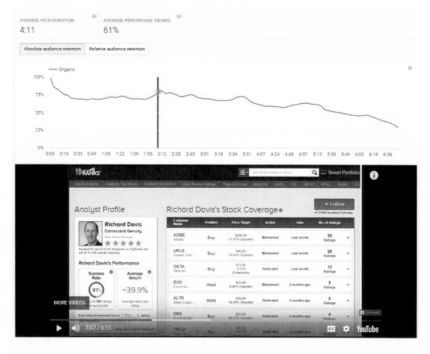

The retention graph for each video will show you where people are lovin' your content and where...not so much. You'll get immediate ideas for making your next video even better.

- There will always be a steep drop initially from casual YouTube surfers and maybe audiences that didn't mean to click on the video. If this initial drop-off lasts more than half a minute or is particularly bad, make sure your video content matches what you promised with the title and thumbnail.

- Look for spikes in the retention, where people are reengaged with the video and might even be playing the section again. For my own videos, these are often where I have graphics or screen shares for a more interactive video.

- Remember to compare the overall retention across videos of similar lengths. Longer videos will naturally have a lower retention because fewer people will have the patience to watch.

- If your videos have a particularly bad drop-off in the last 30 seconds or so, make sure you're not making 'summary' language that signals the video is soon over.

- Look through the videos with higher- and lower-than-normal retention to get ideas for what you're doing right or what could be improved.

Increase Your YouTube CTR by Knowing What Works

Your click-through-rates are the other half of your watch-time but can be extremely frustrating for creators. This is the percentage of people that see your video on their feed, in suggested videos or in search that click on it.

A higher CTR is a powerful signal to YouTube that your video deserves to be pushed out to more people and will result in longer watch-time for the platform.

Finding the click-through-rates on your videos is available in the individual video analytics or by looking at your Top Videos in the Studio. You can also download the data for all videos into a spreadsheet.

YouTube has said, officially, that 80% of creators have CTR between 2% to 10% on average. It's a welcome benchmark but I've never found anyone with an average above 7% click-through. Most of the creators I know are happy with an average somewhere around 5% and ecstatic with a CTR of 6% to 7% on individual videos.

Just like your other metrics, active comparisons are your goal on CTR. Constantly look to your high- and low-CTR videos to see if there are differences you can spot. Test out different ideas over a group of videos to fine-tune your click-through strategy.

- Flat color backgrounds versus images on thumbnails
- Text on thumbnails and different colors for text
- Numerical titles (i.e. 5 Ways to...) versus titles with no numbers
- Different facial expressions for thumbnails

On videos with a very low CTR, you might also consider changing the thumbnail after a week or two. This doesn't change the meta-data to the video so won't reset the momentum but it might just boost your CTR and views.

Video	Views		Watch time (minutes)		Impressions click through rate ⓘ
Total	321,918	100.0%	1,961,225	100.0%	4.3%
10 Best Side Hustle Ideas: How I Made $600 in One Day	91,430	28.4%	688,382	35.1%	5.4%
How to Get Rich Quick in 2019 [3 Short-term Investments]	22,467	7.0%	134,804	6.9%	5.9%
🔍 5 Credit Score Hacks to Boost Your FICO 100 Points	28,966	9.0%	128,144	6.5%	2.3%
Passive Income Dividends: Pay Your Bills with Monthly	26,463	8.2%	127,283	6.5%	6.0%
3 Passive Income Business Ideas [Start with No Money]	20,032	6.2%	99,632	5.1%	5.9%
3 Best Monthly Dividend Stocks for Passive Income	14,510	4.5%	94,097	4.8%	5.9%
5 Best Dividend Stocks to Buy in 2019 [6%+ Dividend Yie...	9,580	3.0%	57,794	2.9%	4.2%
5 Best Short-Term Investments 2019 [Up $20K in 2 Mon...	8,765	2.7%	51,108	2.6%	7.9%
10-Stock Dividend Income Portfolio Thrashing the Mark...	9,200	2.9%	50,968	2.6%	5.2%

Who is Your Audience?

The demographic information about your viewers is not only an opportunity to improve and reach new audiences but also a powerful tool with sponsors.

You can find the age groups, gender and location of people watching your videos by going to your Analytics then Build an Audience.

Your demographics will tell you exactly who your target audience is, the people with whom you're resonating with through the content. This is great information for understanding their particular needs and dreams to deliver hyper-focused videos.

It can also uncover opportunities to reach out to new audiences. For example, my audience skews very much to the male demographic. There's an opportunity there, even if it's difficult to implement, to nearly double my reach by finding ways to appeal to the female half of the audience.

Sponsors and marketers love this demographic data and being able to show your influence with a specific segment. Whether it be males, females or people of a certain age range, you'll find brands trying to reach that group and ready to pay you to do it.

YouTube Traffic Sources Provide a Gold Mine for Content Strategy

The traffic sources that lead to your videos is not only a resource for improvement but also a great way to refine your content strategy. Click on the Reach Viewers tab in your Analytics then click to see more on Traffic Source Types.

Video	Traffic source	Geography	Viewer age	Viewer gender	Revenue source	Subscription status

Traffic source	Impressions click-through rate ⓘ	Views	Average view duration
☐ Total	4.3%	321,918 100.0%	6:05
☐ Browse features	3.7%	138,982 43.2%	5:19
☐ Suggested videos	5.8%	86,632 26.9%	8:05
☐ YouTube search	5.5%	52,062 16.2%	5:13
☐ Channel pages	2.8%	13,930 4.3%	5:18
☐ Other YouTube features	n/a	9,302 2.9%	7:43
☐ External	n/a	6,609 2.1%	4:28
☐ Direct or unknown	n/a	6,508 2.0%	4:22
☐ Notifications	n/a	3,471 1.1%	4:40
☐ Playlists	4.4%	1,909 0.6%	6:36

Your biggest traffic sources will change as your channel grows and matures. For newer channels, Browse features are usually the biggest source though Suggested and Search will slowly grow to a larger proportion of your views.

You can click on the highlighted sources to dig deeper into the information.

Within Suggested Videos are the videos that your channel is being promoted as related. Here you want to ask yourself if there are any channels that are regularly related to yours? YouTube sees the two channels as highly related and making similar videos to the other channel's best videos might just get yours suggested for a breakout in views.

Within YouTube Search are the keywords and phrases that bring you traffic. Look for topics and themes across several keywords. YouTube is telling you that it sees your channel as an authority on these topics. Making additional videos in that topic or theme could do well.

Where's Your Subscriber Growth Coming?

Your most popular videos are the ones that will generally account for the majority of your subscriber growth...but that's not the best information you can get here.

By clicking on Subscribers in your Analytics then clicking through to the YouTube Watch Page data, you can see the subscriber count for each video. You can then download the information into a spreadsheet with views and subscriber gain.

More than just your most popular videos, this is important because you can get a sense for subscribers per view for each topic you cover. Finding a topic or theme that results in massive subscriber growth, even if it doesn't get as many views as others, is a gold-mine for your content strategy. This is your wheelhouse, where you're really connecting with people.

Using analytics to grow a YouTube channel doesn't have to be like sitting through that ninth-grade stats class. This is a real opportunity to understand your viewers and videos to grow faster. None of these analytics are particularly deep or difficult. Have fun with it! Dig in and know that every minute you spend here WILL be rewarded.

Action Steps:
- Navigate to each of the analytics talked about in the chapter and review your own channel. Watch for general trends, strengths and weaknesses.
- Don't spend too much time on your analytics. Set a schedule to review your analytics every couple of weeks. Look for trends and opportunities but don't lose time spending hours looking at analytics every day.

HOW TO PROMOTE YOUR YOUTUBE VIDEOS WITH A BLOG AND SOCIAL MEDIA

Using a blog and social media to promote your YouTube channel leverages the power of multiple platforms for huge business growth

I talked to a YouTube creator a few months ago that was just starting his blog...after more than five years as a creator and 50,000 subscribers!

It struck me as a huge missed opportunity. The creator had no email list, no community off YouTube and was struggling to keep subscribers coming back to the videos.

Fast-forward to last week, the creator had turned their new blog into a revenue source making over $3,000 a month in addition to his YouTube income. The average number of views on each video has almost doubled and he's now at almost 100,000 subscribers!

Even this story of success, leveraging a blog with a YouTube channel, hides some of the biggest reasons every creator should have a blog and social media strategy.

It's not just about promoting your channel but about amplifying your message across platforms and building a community that will follow you anywhere.

Why Should Every YouTube Channel Have a Blog?

When I first started my YouTube channel in 2015, it was simply to have a place to host video summaries of my blog posts. The idea was that I would create two-minute summaries to embed on the blogs that would offer readers another media format and keep them on-page longer, an important signal of quality to Google.

The videos did their job on the blog but did nothing for the YouTube channel. Of course, I didn't really care about the channel so it didn't matter that I only had 22 subscribers by the end of 2017.

When I started using YouTube and my blogs together, leveraging the strength of each for mutual benefit, that's when the real magic happened.

That's when I gained over 36,500 subscribers in a year and am on pace to reach 120,000+ by the end of two years. Using a blog in your YouTube strategy is like having a continuous collaboration, always being able to help each other and grow.

First is through embedding your videos in articles. The current understanding is that if someone watches roughly half of your embedded video off-YT then it counts as a view and watch-time. Of course, this can always change and it's probably the least of the benefits to having a blog.

The real benefit is that you're building a community on both mediums, on your blog and on the channel. Your blog is going to be attracting people from completely different sources like Google search and other blogs. By using the blog and channel together, you'll grow community to each faster.

Having that written content medium with a blog also opens you up to more opportunities for monetization. While a lot of sponsors and advertisers are shifting their budget to video, they still spend the majority to traditional content. By being able to offer sponsors a video and the transcribed blog-post, you effectively double their exposure with little additional work on your part.

Finally, and perhaps most importantly, is the fact that YOU own your blog.

I've got a lot of friends that built their entire business around their Facebook pages and groups. It was an easy solution for years, easy traffic and very little cost. Then Facebook started shifting to a pay-to-play model, limiting the reach of pages unless the owner ran thousands of dollars in ads.

There was nothing anyone could do and many had to start over from scratch.

As an online entrepreneur, one of the most important things you can do is constantly ask yourself, "Where does my money come from?" What are the assets you own and what would happen if sources you don't own changed their business model?

It's part of the reason I diversify my income across seven sources from self-publishing to affiliates and ad revenue. It's also the reason I make money on my own blogs as well as 3rd party platforms like YouTube and Facebook.

How to Use a Blog with Your YouTube Channel

We'll walk through six strategies to using a blog with your YouTube channel. As you read through each and brainstorm other ideas always keep a main goal in mind, how can you use each resource to benefit the other.

That's the main point here. As I learned, it's not about using one site solely to grow the other but using your blog to grow on YouTube and using your channel to grow the blog.

1) First is to add a YouTube subscribe button to the sidebar on your blog

Sidebar items don't result in a tidal wave of clicks but they show on every page and will bring you subscribers. You can also use the button in other places and it's just an easy way of letting people know you're on YouTube as well.

Click through to the Google HTML embed code generator here

- Enter your YouTube username, user ID or channel ID or click 'Retrieve Channel ID' in the left-menu
- Choose the layout for your button
- Google will generate a code to copy that you can paste into a text box in the widgets section of your blog

2) Next we got to our YouTube channel and add a blog link on the About page

We talked about adding links in the previous chapter on setting up a YouTube channel. The links will show at the bottom of your About page and you can designate some to show on your channel banner as well.

For smaller channels just starting out, you might want to limit the number of links you show on your banner. While the idea is to send people to your blog and grow your community, YouTube penalizes channels that send a lot of traffic off-site. It's not a problem for larger channels because you've already got the momentum to keep growing but smaller channels need to be strict with the number of outbound links.

That said, there's nothing wrong with posting a few links on your About page. Link to your blog home page as well as important lead magnets. If someone is interested enough to visit the About section of your channel, they're probably close to becoming part of your community so give them as many options as possible.

3) Transcribe your videos and use them as blog posts

I script all my videos so this is an easy one but might be a little more work if you generally just record from notes. If you don't script your videos, you can always just create a blog post as a summary or hire a freelancer to transcribe the video.

As we talked about in our post on making money on YouTube, transcribing your videos gives sponsors another touch-point with the audience. That's a great selling-point to pitch sponsors that aren't yet sure about video or haven't allocated much of a budget. They get twice the work from their sponsorship dollars.

Of course the best part about creating blog posts around each video is that you can embed the video and promote your YouTube channel. You get twice the work from each video with no more effort. Take it from someone that runs four blogs and a YouTube channel, it's a huge time-saver.

- Write a brief introduction to the post before embedding the video. Something to warm people up and tell them what they'll learn.

- I like to embed the video right after this introduction. Video is something most blogs don't offer so it's a nice added feature. You can embed your video at the end of the post but many readers might not even see it.

- Immediately below the video embed, write out a few sentences on what you talk about on the channel and why people should subscribe. Then link your subscribe code so that people clicking over will automatically be asked if they want to subscribe.

- You'll need to edit some parts of your video transcript, specifically the callouts where you reference a link in the video description. You'll also want to add on-page SEO points like section headings and internal links.

- Promote your blog post just as you would any other post.

Maybe the biggest benefit to putting your videos up as blog posts is that extra first-day boost to your videos. I upload the transcribed post before the video goes live and just schedule the blog post to publish a couple hours later. This gives me time to grab the embed code or URL for the video and update the post.

4) Reference blog posts in your videos and add links in the description

Within six months of developing my YouTube channel, visitors from the video site were within the top five traffic sources. Not only that but they stayed longer and clicked through more pages that any other traffic source.

All Web Site Data ▾

	Source / Medium	Acquisition				Behavior		
		Sessions ↓	% New Sessions	New Users		Bounce Rate	Pages / Session	Avg. Session Duration
		74,798	85.99%	64,322		89.25%	1.18	00:00:46
☐	1. google / organic	47,461 (63.45%)	86.49%	41,047 (63.81%)		90.80%	1.15	00:00:45
☐	2. (direct) / (none)	10,858 (14.52%)	81.64%	8,864 (13.78%)		84.62%	1.27	00:00:48
☐	3. pinterest.com / referral	7,836 (10.48%)	91.45%	7,166 (11.14%)		90.75%	1.14	00:00:43
☐	4. pinterest.com / social	1,907 (2.55%)	91.77%	1,750 (2.72%)		89.09%	1.15	00:00:55
☐	5. youtube.com / referral	1,357 (1.81%)	71.04%	964 (1.50%)		81.80%	1.33	00:01:22
☐	6. bing / organic	634 (0.85%)	91.32%	579 (0.90%)		89.27%	1.18	00:00:45

Of course, the preference is usually going to be to reference one of your other videos and keep people on YouTube. This will make it more likely they'll subscribe to your channel and helps trigger the YouTube algorithm to show your videos to more people.

But if you have a blog post that's relevant and you don't have a video you can reference, mention the post and that you'll provide a link in the video description.

I see an average of 5% click-through on video description links that I reference in a video. That means about 50 visitors to your blog for every 1,000 people that view the video. Get a video to go viral with a few hundred thousand views and you've got thousands of visitors to your blog.

5) Add links to your lead magnets in every video description

There are three or four paragraphs I add to the bottom of every video description.

- A paragraph about the channel and why people should join the community by subscribing, followed by the auto-subscribe link.
- A paragraph leading into my investing course funnel with a link to my free webinar.
- A paragraph and link to a lead magnet related to the video's content.
- A paragraph about me and my story

That link to the lead magnet has brought me thousands of email subscribers and multiples of that in affiliate sales and course purchases.

A lead magnet is just a brief, one- to five-page, printable that goes into detail on a topic. This might be something like a checklist or quick bulleted guide to a process. You offer this free to email subscribers on the blog to get people into your community.

*Important: Remember, you don't want to change the video description after it's already published. This will reset the metadata and the video's view momentum could suffer. Just add these links to new videos you post.

How to Promote a YouTube Channel on Social Media

While social media can be a big source of visitors for a new YouTube channel, managing multiple platforms and doing everything you need to engage can feel overwhelming. To that I would say, don't feel like you need to be on EVERY social media platform. In fact, you could be wasting your time if you try being on too many.

One of the biggest mistakes bloggers and YouTube creators make is the shotgun approach to social media. They link their new videos in a post on six different platforms and wonder why they never get any traffic from social.

The problem is, they're not being...SOCIAL!

Social media is about engaging, building a relationship with people and the trust it takes for them to regularly care about what you're saying. Simply spamming pages and groups with your links leads to worse than nothing because you're actually building a bad reputation.

The rate of engagement; that's clicks, comments and likes per number of people that see a post, is tragically low on social media. Engagement with the average post on Facebook is just 0.17%... and that's higher than most other platforms. On average just one person out of 600 that see a post are engaging with it through a like, click or comment. On Twitter, it's as low as 0.05% and just as bad on Pinterest and LinkedIn.

It's much better to choose two or three social platforms on which you can really build a community. We'll go over some strategy and how to do that for four platforms below but the overall idea will be the same.

- Start a conversation with people
- Answer questions and become a resource
- Draw them to your blog or YouTube videos
- Repeat regularly

Build that relationship with your followers on social media and you can see engagement rates as high as 2% on your posts. That might not seem like much but it means you get someone engaging with your post for every 50 people that see it rather than needing 600 people to see it.

Using Facebook to Promote a YouTube Channel

Facebook is the powerhouse in social media and almost obligatory for anyone with an online business. With more than two billion users globally, your audience can be found on the social network.

I say ALMOST obligatory because you could build a huge community on any of the other platforms. Even SnapChat with its relatively tiny platform still has over 250 million users. The moral here is to use whichever platform you enjoy and feel like you can most efficiently and effectively reach people.

For a lot of people, Facebook still fits within that mantra. Most people have an account so the learning curve to using Facebook is faster than trying to learn how another platform works.

Understand though that Facebook hates sending people off-site. All social platforms want to keep users on the platform but Facebook is probably the most ruthless at how it guards its traffic.

In the past several years, this has meant limiting the reach of posts that include a link to another site. Facebook has also been limiting the reach of pages and groups, turning the platform into a pay-to-play model for anyone trying to reach an audience.

The work-around to much of this has recently been to place the link to your YouTube video in the first comment of a post and calling attention to it in the post. That worked for a while to get the post shown to more people but it seems Facebook is now limiting the reach of posts with links in comments as well.

All this just means you need a defined strategy for promoting your YouTube channel on Facebook and the flexibility to evolve it as Facebook changes.

A Basic Facebook Strategy for YouTube

- Day One: Share a post with your video link. You can do this on your page, within your personal feed and where it's relevant in groups in which you engage. Understand that a link will auto-populate your video that will play directly on Facebook. Instead, upload your thumbnail as an image and then add your link to make it clickable and send people to YouTube.
- Day Two: Share a 30- to 45-second clip of your video directly on Facebook and add a link to the whole video on YouTube.
- Day Three: Do a quick Facebook Live to talk about key points in the video and reference your link in the first comment.
- Day Four: Ask a question related to the video topic on your Facebook page and reference the video with a link in the first comment.

Do this on a regular schedule and it will give you maximum exposure for each video as well as build a community directly on Facebook.

Using Twitter to Promote a YouTube Channel

Twitter may not have the reach as Facebook with 'only' 355 million users but it's a relatively easy platform to promote your YouTube channel. Understand that the lifespan of a tweet is very much shorter than a Facebook post and that's going to guide your strategy.

For example, followers on Facebook might see your post for days after you publish and pins on Pinterest can be found for years. By comparison, it's estimated that a tweet gets buried in a user's feed within eight minutes of posting.

This means you need to post continuously to make sure people have the opportunity to see your update. Even posting as much as ten times a day doesn't guarantee that all your followers will see your tweet.

- Tweet at least three times on Day One of your video
- Schedule to promote the video at least twice more over the next week and each month thereafter

To avoid annoying users with the same post, you need to change it up with each tweet. You can use quotes from the video, interesting data or graphics as well as list ideas. Anything to draw attention to the tweet in a different way.

You'll have the same linking problem on Twitter as we saw on Facebook so consider uploading your thumbnail image first and then the link so people are redirected to YouTube rather than watch the video on Twitter.

Using Pinterest to Promote a YouTube Channel

Pinterest is a different sort of animal compared to the other social platforms. In fact, it's really more of a search engine than it is a social network. There are some advantages as well as disadvantages to that when it comes to promoting your YouTube channel.

Because it's a search engine, your shared video or pin doesn't die as quickly as it does on Facebook or Twitter. If a pin starts showing well for a search term, you can get traffic from it for years after posting.

On the downside, it can be difficult to build a community on Pinterest like you would on other networks. With Pinterest, it's every pin for itself. Disadvantages aside, I would have to say that Pinterest is probably the one social media platform everyone needs to be on.

I avoided the platform for years. I thought my blog content wasn't visual and I didn't want to commit myself to a new social platform. It was only after hearing from blogger friends how they were drawing hundreds of thousands of visitors from the site every month that I though, "Maybe there's something to this Pinterest thing."

Now I've never hit that 100K+ success on Pinterest but within a few months it had grown to my second-largest traffic source to the blogs. Whether you're promoting a blog or a YouTube channel, Pinterest can send you thousands of visitors every month.

- Understand the type of pin, both style and format that works best on Pinterest. This means creating a long, portrait-style image for each video that you can use on the platform.

- You can include a description of up to 500 characters for each pin but a few hundred characters is a good target. This is going to help your pin show up in search and rank for certain keywords. You'll also want to use hashtags for a few keywords important to your pin.

- Pin to one of your boards on the first day your video is published.

- Pin to group boards over the next two days

- Join Pinterest groups on Facebook or just reach out to other creators on Pinterest to share each other's pins.

Using Instagram to Promote a YouTube Channel

Instagram is quickly becoming a powerhouse in social media with more than 100 million users. Since it's owned by Facebook, you're likely to see all the problems of linking and reach here as well. In fact, Instagram doesn't even allow links in individual posts until you reach 10,000 followers so it's all about building a community that will follow you.

Instagram is much more a visual platform than Facebook. Similar to Pinterest, this means you need to put more time in creating the images that will get clicks and followers. Images should be a square format so they show without cropping and don't necessarily need text.

As with all social posts you make, a call-to-action is important to tell people what you want them to do. We're so used to just scrolling through our social feed that most don't even think about clicking through to watch a video or get more information. Your last sentence in every social post should be an explicit request for the reader to do something.

Since Instagram is all about building a community, diversity of shares is important. Create a schedule for sharing quotes, lists, funny pics and other ideas besides just drawing attention to your new videos.

Taking your channel off YouTube is one of the best ways to go beyond the normal creator and really grow your channel. The vast majority of creators spend less than an hour a week, spamming their video link on different sites and never really building a community. Not only will a blogging and social strategy help you leverage communities on different platforms but it will diversify your income sources for true business growth.

Action Steps:

- You can create a simple blog in less than an hour. I know it's a lot of work to create a blog AND a YouTube channel at the same time but just put together a basic website you can use to promote your channel. I share a free checklist to starting a blog here.

- Create a page for your YouTube channel on at least two social media platforms

- Outline the strategy you will follow to promote your videos and grow a following on those social platforms

MAKING MONEY ON YOUTUBE: HOW I MADE OVER $25,000 IN YEAR ONE

Learning how to make money on YouTube is much more than just using ads on your videos

In less than a year, YouTube has grown to half of my online income. That's not because income from my four blogs or 10 self-published books have fallen but simply the speed and power of making money on YouTube.

You can make a LOT of money on YouTube!

But like running a blog or other online businesses, you need to understand the potential income sources and how to use each if you're going to make real money. Waiting around for Google, YouTube's parent company and ad network, to make you rich is going to be a very long wait.

Building a multi-stream approach to making money on YouTube will not only make you as much as possible but will also smooth out the ups-and-downs so you've got an income every single month.

Let's look at six income sources for YouTube creators, the pros and cons of each, and how to get started making a steady paycheck for your videos.

Here are the income sources I'll talk about as well as how to put them all together.

- Sponsorships
- Affiliates
- Own Products
- YouTube Ads
- SuperChat
- Patreon

The Right Way to Make Money on YouTube

Click through to almost any "How Much Did I Make on YouTube" video and the conversation is almost entirely about how much the creator made in ads. This leads to the general feeling that ads are THE ONLY way to make money on YouTube.

Since ad income is so low…that leads to the general opinion, and a lot of blog posts, that creators don't make much money on the platform.

Maybe it's just coming over from years of blogging that I knew, if I was ever going to make money on YouTube, it would have to be with other sources rather than just ads. Google ads on a blog pay very little, around $14 per thousand impressions, while even the better ad networks usually only get you around $24 per thousand impressions.

That means you need tens of thousands of page views to make any amount of money…and it's even worse for YouTube ads.

I was able to start monetizing my videos with ads on June 26th, almost exactly six months from starting the channel. Monthly video views were around 150,000 so the channel was growing quickly but that still only translated into about $1,500 for the month.

I made just over $9,000 over the first six months of YouTube ads on around 800,000 views over the period.

That number doesn't even compare to the $16,000 I made in sponsorships and affiliates over the period and those got started months later than ads…and I've only just started selling my own courses and books through videos.

If you want to make money on YouTube, you need a strategy for making money through multiple sources!

We'll start with my three favorite sources; sponsorships, affiliates and own products. Own products will generally make you the most money if you can develop the marketing funnel around them but they also take the most time. Affiliates are probably the easiest. Sponsorships come a little later after you've built a community but can be big money as well.

Making Money through Sponsorships

Athletes do it. Movie and TV stars do it. Anyone with a handful of followers on social media seems to be getting sponsors.

As a YouTube creator, one of your biggest income sources will be sponsorships from companies (brands).

Sponsorships tend to come in three types,

- A fee for producing a video or series of videos
- A base fee plus commission on clicks or sales for a video or series
- Free products for the creator

Free products are nice and can be significant compensation,

especially for smaller channels that might not yet be able to get much in a direct fee, but I want to concentrate here on making money for your channel.

If you are interested in getting free products, watch videos on similar channels to see what they review or just look to the products/services available in your niche. Make a list and go to companies' websites to find contact information. Then tell them you'd very much like to try their product to review it on the channel if they would send you a sample or sign you up for a trial service.

Always check any existing deals or discounts they have on the product and ask for more than this. After all, you need to be getting something extra for your efforts.

Getting paid to do a video is the ultimate validation of your channel. You've joined the professional TV and movie producers...but how do you get to that point?

- Use the same approach as getting free products. See what other channels are promoting and visit blogs in your niche. Look for a Resources Page to see what is most often recommended.

- Conferences can be a great way to find sponsors. If the company is willing to pay for a booth at a conference, they've got a marketing budget and might be willing to do a deal.

- It helps to have some hard data to pitch the value of your channel so I'd recommend doing a few videos promoting some affiliates first. Use a link tracking tool like the PrettyLink plugin to give you data on the click-through-rate (CTR). You'll know the video views and will get conversion data from the affiliate program. These three points will help prove what you can bring to a sponsor.

There are two types of videos you can do for a sponsor.

The first is a general interest video related to the sponsor. For example you might do a video on repayment plans available for student loans in a sponsorship with a student loan refinance company. You mention the sponsor a couple of times, talking about using them as an option and features of the company.

General interest videos have the benefit of appealing to a much larger audience and not coming across as a commercial. You're still providing valuable information through the video's content. The audience appreciates the content and gets the sponsor pitch on a more subconscious-level.

The other type of sponsored video is a direct review of the product or service. This is popular in the 'unboxing' theme or just reviewing a company's website and service.

The benefit to review videos is that they are generally easier to rank for that keyword and have a higher CTR and conversion rate. This makes sense because anyone clicking onto a video titled 'Company XYZ Review' is probably already interested in the company or at least aware of the problem they need solved.

The best strategy is actually a mix of these two types of videos [and I feel like I'm giving away one of my biggest secrets here].

When I approach a sponsor, I like to pitch for a series of videos including two general interest videos and one review.

The campaign starts with the two general interest videos to draw in as many viewers as possible and warm them up to the idea of the company's product or service. The third video, the direct review, benefits from more views and an audience that is already aware of their problem and recognizes the company's brand.

This is not only a great way to get more conversions for your sponsors but also a persuasive way to sell the sponsorship to the company. Most of the people you talk to will be from the old school of marketing, relying on blanketing TV with multiple commercials to build brand recognition. They love hearing how your campaign idea 'warms up' an audience and offers those multiple touch-points.

Of course, I also like the strategy because you get paid for three videos instead of just one!

Each video includes a link to the company in your video description. I like to include in the pitch that I transcribe the videos and upload as a blog post as well to give the company double the exposure. Of course, I don't tell them how easy this is because I script all my videos or that I put most of my videos up as blog posts anyway because it helps trigger the YouTube algorithm.

How much you charge your sponsors will depend on your niche and how many conversions typically come from videos. Here's a good way to find how much to charge,

- Look at how much affiliates in the industry are offering per lead or conversion
- Find the median (not the average because it's skewed by high-view videos) view count for your videos over the last month or two
- If you have data on click-through-rates and conversions for your videos through affiliates you've highlighted then you can use that. Otherwise, a good rule-of-thumb is a CTR of around 5% - 10% and a similar conversion rate on your videos.
- You can also look to see how much advertisers are paying Google Adwords for clicks on a certain keyword
- This will give you an idea of how many conversions or clicks you might expect to the sponsor from your video and how much to charge them.

For example:

- A related affiliate to the potential sponsor offers $50 commission for each conversion or you also find that advertisers on Google Adwords are paying about $4 per click for a related keyword.
- You get approximately 1,000 views on your videos
- You estimate that 6% of viewers will click through the sponsored link in your video description and about 5% of these will end up buying the product. It's always better if this data comes directly from other campaigns you've done but an estimate will work too.
- 1,000 views times 6% means 60 clicks and 5% of that means 3 conversions
- A sponsor would expect to pay around $150 for those three conversions ($50 times three) or $240 for the clicks on a pay-per-click ad campaign.

I've also seen creators talk about charging an average of between $0.05 to $0.15 per views you typically get on a video. As a numbers nerd, I like the procedural estimate better and sponsors respond more favorably when you can prove some estimate of value.

Some sponsors will try talking you into only accepting a commission on sales through an affiliate program. I will generally drop my fee a little if an affiliate program is included, so I stand to make more money with commissions, but I always charge a base fee as well. Explain to the sponsor that you stand behind your videos and know they convert but production costs for video are so much higher than a simple blog post that you need a base fee to cover some of those up-front expenses.

I always ask for at least half the total fee upfront before I start work on a campaign and then the remaining payment payable after the final video is published. If the sponsorship is for just one video, then the entire fee is paid upfront.

By law and YouTube terms, you need to disclose whenever you receive compensation from a sponsorship. You should do this both verbally in the video as well as through YouTube's sponsor declaration in the video's 'Advanced Settings".

- I like to add in the lead-up to the video content something like, "I put this video together in partnership with XYZ company," or "...in partnership with XYZ company, I want to show you..."
- When you're uploading the video, go to Advanced Settings and click on the Content Declaration box.
- Checking the box marked 'Help me inform viewers...' isn't usually required but you can check YouTube's disclosure rules. Checking this will put a small text box "Includes Paid Promotion" in the lower-left of your video for the first minute.

Making Money with Affiliates on YouTube

Affiliate commissions account for the bulk of my income on the blogs, around 45% to 60% some months, but seem to be less on YouTube. Part of that is probably because I focus more on sponsorships for the channel than only on affiliates.

I might do a few videos including affiliates if I think they will convert especially well or if I can include a few different affiliates into one video idea, but generally I like to try getting a sponsorship fee plus commissions if I'm going to be talking about a company.

It means MORE MONEY!

Your strategy for promoting affiliates can work in much the same way you approach sponsored videos, mentioning affiliate products in general interest videos as well as directly reviewing the company. There are a few points I'd recommend on finding affiliates and monetizing your videos.

- If you don't have a blog [you absolutely should because it's a great complement to your channel] to tell you which affiliates convert the best for your audience, look to related channels and blogs to see what they promote.

- Don't waste your time with unrelated affiliate links in the video description. Anytime you're planning on sending someone off YouTube through a link, ask yourself if it's really worth it. YouTube doesn't like when people click out of its site so you better be building a list or monetizing that traffic for it to be worth the potential hit to your video.

- It's up to you whether you do a call-out of the affiliate in the video, mentioning the link in the description, or just place the link. I try to reference at least one other video and tell people to look for the link in every video so that at least gets them looking in the video description, potentially clicking on the affiliate as well.

- Just as in blogging, list posts work great and can be an excellent way to make money. Put a video together in a theme where you can include or compare five or more affiliates and other companies. Make it impartial and just focus on providing valuable content, then add all your affiliate links in the description.

Despite the potential hit from the algorithm for having an outbound link in your video description, I would recommend you try to include at least one related affiliate in most videos. You never know which video is going to blow up and you don't want to change the description after it already has. You'll kick yourself later if there was a perfect affiliate you could have included in a video that ends up getting a million views.

Selling Your Own Products on YouTube

Selling your own products on YouTube makes a lot of sense.

First, you have nobody taking a share of the profits. With affiliate sales, not only is the company going to take their cut but also the affiliate network. With sponsorships, you're selling another company's product for a small percentage of what a customer is worth to them.

I have friends that charge $1,000 and even $10,000 for a course. That's a lot of money compared to the typical $50 payout for an affiliate sale.

Selling your own products also works well because people on your channel are more likely to trust you or you at least have some brand recognition. They've seen your videos, know that you try giving them the best information you can, and that trust carries over to your products.

This can translate to a lot of money from dozens of different product ideas,

- Merchandise like t-shirts and mugs with your logo or interesting quotes printed on them
- Mastermind groups, weekly or bi-weekly meetings with you and a group of people
- One-on-One consulting
- Books and Video Courses

There are two drawbacks to selling your own products that you need to consider.

It sucks but it's not enough to create a great product. You have to market it and get it in front of people. In fact, as someone that's created multiple courses and books, I'd say marketing is 75% or more of the work.

That means you'll also need to develop a marketing funnel through which to sell your products. It might not be necessary if you're just selling a $10 t-shirt but if you're trying to get $100 or more for a course, you'll need to warm people up to the idea.

- You can use videos to draw people in and offer a free webinar
- Pre-webinar emails can warm them up to the solution of a problem they share
- Through the webinar, you give them as much value as possible to grow that trust factor, then pitch a special offer on your course or other product
- Post-webinar emails drive home the value of the product and special offer

This is a pretty typical example of a marketing funnel but there are other things you can do including using Facebook or YouTube ads. Typical conversion rates are about 20% to 30% of your webinar sign-ups will actually show up and between 5% to 10% of those will end up purchasing.

Doing the math on that, and you can see you need a lot of video views to produce sales. For example, if 15% of your video views click to the webinar signup and 30% of those register, then 25%

show up and 10% end up buying...you need just under 900 video views for each purchase.

The second drawback of selling your own products is the time and effort it takes compared to other sources like sponsorships and affiliates. You need to consider the time developing and managing your products as part of the costs.

If you're selling a course, that means developing the course and marketing. It also means managing the sales process and students in the course.

None of this is to say that your own products aren't a great money-maker on YouTube. I'm just getting started selling my courses through the platform and it's been worth it so far. Just understand it's not the get-rich idea that some would have you believe.

Just one warning about selling your courses, merchandise or other products on YouTube...don't make it ALL about the sales. I see so many creators spend years to build up a community then alienate everyone with continuous pitches to buy everything from t-shirts and courses. I'll talk more about this later in the chapter but moderate your sales pitches and make sure you're always providing quality information.

Making Money on YouTube Ads

Despite not paying much compared to other income sources, YouTube has a great system set up in their ads platform. This is where the bulk of most creators' income comes from though we've seen already that maybe it shouldn't be.

Once you're approved for the YouTube partner program, the platform will start showing ads on your videos. To get accepted into the program, you need over 1,000 subscribers and 4,000 total watch-hours over the last twelve months.

Once you meet these requirements, it might take a couple of months to get approved but then the ads will start appearing automatically.

That's the great part about YouTube ads. After a few minutes applying and setting things up, everything is done for you.

This is easily done by going to Creator Studio → Channel Settings → Monetization

First 'Apply to the Partner Program' which is just a one-click action. You'll see your watch-hours here as well as whether you qualify on the subscriber count basis.

- You'll need to open a Google Adsense account and associate it with your channel. This is how you'll be paid as well, with a monthly ACH deposit or check. You also need to tell YouTube which ads you want to show on your videos.

- Go to the Monetization Settings to tell YouTube what kind of ads you want to show

Here are the types of ads YouTube currently uses,

- Overlay in-video ads are transparent boxes of ads shown on lower part of video

- Skippable video ads come on before your video and skippable after a few seconds

- Non-skippable video ads

- Sponsored cards are notes appearing in the upper-right just like your own cards

- Automatic mid-roll ads are video ads that interrupt your video after a certain amount of time

- Display ads are shown to the right of your video in the sidebar and are always turned on.

Most of my ad revenue (85%) will come from Skippable video ads, usually followed by about 11% from Display ads and 2.3% from

Bumper Ads. I've turned off non-skippable ads though they tend to pay higher rates, I just don't like the idea of forcing viewers to sit through a 15-second or longer ad.

I've also turned off the mid-roll ads on my videos. Most people don't think anything of commercials during a TV show but it's still a little off-putting to see a YouTube video interrupted for an ad. You'll see viewer drop-offs increase during ads but it still might be something to consider if you're not monetizing much through the other income sources. After all, more ads means more money!

You can also turn monetization off for individual videos. You might do this on a sponsored video if the partner requests it though I usually keep it turned on for all videos.

YouTube gives creators 55% of the ad revenue it collects from advertisers on your videos. The actual amount you will earn depends on your niche. Some niche like personal finance, investing and education tend to pay higher rates while other niche like beauty or kids toys pay a little less. It just depends on what YouTube is able to get from advertisers.

I've seen rates that translate to about $0.0035 per view for some channels, mostly in those lower-paying niches, while my income and other channels in personal finance average $0.01 per view on ad-monetized videos.

Other Ways to Make Money on YouTube

There are two more ways creators are making money on YouTube, both with their pros and cons. I haven't used either but have spent a good deal of time researching each and talking with others using them.

SuperChat is a viewer sponsorship during live streams. Basically it's like a donation the viewer gives you for doing a good job. The viewer 'buys' a superchat, usually from $5 and up, and you receive a notification in the comment section during the live stream.

YouTube takes 30% of your Super Chat revenue and passes the remaining on to you through your Adsense account.

The upside to a Super Chat for viewers, beyond supporting their favorite channels, is that it highlights their comment and is usually a good way to get their question answered or an appreciative shout-out from the creator.

Some creators like to make a little pitch for super chat payments occasionally during a live stream and thanking others for their Super Chat always helps to bring out a few more. It's only available through live streams so if you're not doing these, it won't be much of an income source.

Besides the fact that I don't often do live streams, YouTube's 30% take on something it really doesn't have to do anything turns me off the source. Live streams can be a good way to connect with the community though so this might be a bigger part of your YouTube income.

Patreon is another popular income source for creators. The website is based on the old system of patronage that's used with artists and other creatives. This is where someone will support an artist with a monthly income in exchange for rights or just to enjoy the works they create.

This system has given us some of the most beautiful renaissance works and paintings from Michelangelo and Botticelli. Applying it to YouTube is an interesting idea and can be significant income.

YouTube creators start a page on Patreon and offer extras to patrons in tiers. These might include early access to videos, exclusive videos or behind-the-scenes, group meetings or really anything extra. Patrons sign up for a tier, a specific charge, and that amount is deducted monthly until they stop.

From the patronage fees to your profile, Patreon takes:
- A 5% fee on all money collected from Patrons
- A processing fee around 3% charged to Patrons
- A payout fee of between $0.25 to $20 to transfer your money to a bank account, PayPal or Payoneer

For example, Ross Tran offers five tiers ranging from monthly patronage of $1 to $100 for different benefits in each. He's got over 1,000 patrons so is making anywhere from $1,039 to $103,900 per month depending on what tiers his average patron is choosing.

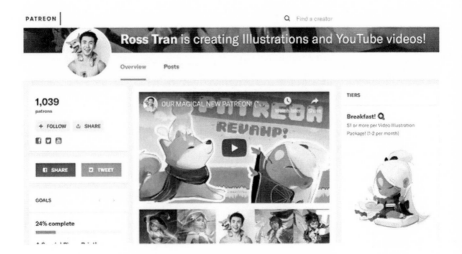

The problem I have with Patreon isn't the amount charged by the platform which is well under what YouTube takes on its Super Chat program. It just doesn't seem to be much money compared to other income sources.

Case in point, Ross Tran has over 800,000 subscribers on YouTube but only a thousand patrons. Another popular YouTube creator that actively promotes his Patreon page, Tim Schmoyer, has over 450,000 subscribers but only 151 patrons.

It can still be a lot of money if you're able to get people over to your Patreon page and offer some exciting benefits for monthly support...to me it just doesn't seem like it's worth the effort to manage versus some of the other income sources.

YouTube has launched its own membership feature directly on the platform where viewers can support a channel on a monthly basis. Like many YouTube features, the program is constantly evolving but currently you need more than 30,000 subscribers to qualify.

The program works very similar to the Patreon model except you run into the same problem as the SuperChat function with YouTube taking 30% of the donated amount. I appreciate YouTube coming out with new ways for creators to make money but that's a deal-breaker for me.

The warning I pointed out in selling your own products applies to all income sources so it's worth repeating. Turning your videos into constant commercials and sales pitches will drive away your community and cause your growth to stagnate.

There's no rule for how many of your videos can be directly monetized, i.e. sponsored or product-focused, without turning off subscribers. I like to keep it under a fifth or a third of the videos published. This doesn't mean you can't add an affiliate link to each video description, it just means I try not to make a sales pitch or referral within the video content for more than a third of the videos.

It's also the reason I like doing general interest videos where I can provide quality information while still calling out an affiliate or sponsor rather than just a direct review of a product. Viewers are much more accepting of a monetized video if they're getting some great information that helps them whether they buy a product or not.

Making money on YouTube isn't the get-rich scheme some creators make it out to be but it also isn't the slow grind of making pennies per video on ads. Learn how to integrate different income sources into your content strategy and your videos will continue making money years after you've published. Spend the time to understand YouTube as a business and you WILL be rewarded!

Action Steps

- Outline a business plan for making money on your YouTube channel. List out each income source and how you might use it.

- Review similar channels and blogs and list out the companies they promote and use on their 'Resources' page. These are prime targets for sponsorships or affiliates.

- Join at least a couple of Ad Networks like CJ Affiliates and Impact Radius. Browse their list of brands to see which are most relevant to your channel niche.

- List out a few ideas for your own products whether it be self-publishing a book, a course, consulting or other ideas.

- Partner with a couple of affiliates and plan how you can promote the product through reviews or list videos.

THREE STRATEGIES TO GROW SUBSCRIBERS ON YOUTUBE

Growing subscribers to a YouTube channel is about asking and about building a community around your brand

You can be doing everything right on your YouTube channel, have some great videos and have the channel set up perfectly, and yet people still might not become subscribers.

And it's because you haven't asked them to subscribe!

It seems unnecessary and I know a lot of creators don't want to sound 'pushy' with constant requests for people to join their subscriber community. The fact is that's exactly what it takes to build a subscriber following on YouTube. You have to ask...no you have to tell people to subscribe.

I'm going to reveal three ways to grow your YouTube channel, how to use each and how to turn it into a community of cheerleaders. These ideas work and they're the reason 3% of my viewers turn into subscribers versus a ratio closer to 1.4% or less for most channels.

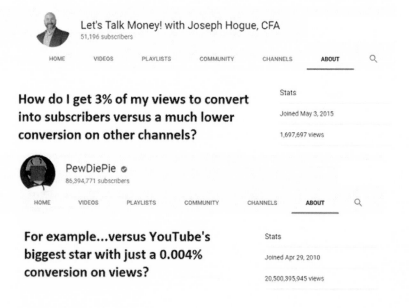

Ask People to Subscribe to Your YouTube Channel…and Ask…and Ask

We'll talk about building a community and giving people a reason to subscribe but the best and easiest way to grow your YouTube subscribers is just to ask.

I understand you don't want to come off as pushy or maybe you reason that if your videos are just so awesome, people shouldn't need to be reminded about subscribing. The fact is, even the best and most professionally-produced channels on YouTube need to remind people that subscribing is even an option.

The problem is that most people still watch YouTube as a how-to platform or just end up there casually to watch the latest cat video. They don't think of the platform as a legitimate alternative to TV. They may not even understand that subscribing to a channel is free or that it helps them find videos that will help them.

People have never needed to 'subscribe' to their favorite TV channels. They've got a guide to tell them what's on and may even know the schedule for a favorite network.

Until it becomes the same way on YouTube, you need to explicitly ask people to subscribe and remind them why they should.

This means placing multiple Calls-to-Action (CTAs) in your videos, both verbally and through text or graphics. Besides just asking people to click the subscribe button, you can tell them why they should and what they get out of it. If you're producing quality videos, this is going to be more of just a reminder though, something to make your viewers sit up and say, "Oh, yeah. I didn't even think about that but good idea."

Here are the subscribe CTAs I use in my videos:

- A verbal welcome and thank you to everyone in the community within the first minute of the video followed by, "If you're not a member of that community yet, just click the subscribe button. It's free and you'll never miss an episode."

- A graphic subscribe button image that appears during my welcome message

- A small subscribe watermark that stays in the lower-right

corner through the video, something we talked about setting up your YouTube channel.

- References to upcoming video topics when relevant and a call to subscribe so viewers don't miss when the video goes live
- The end screen CTA, a subscribe button and text callout on the left-side of the screen and a verbal call to action with, "If you've got a question about money, just subscribe to the channel and ask it in the comments below..."

That gives me three to four requests for subscribers in each video. You better believe, if someone is even thinking about subscribing to the channel, it's going to be in their head.

Making YouTube More than Just a Channel

Asking people to subscribe is one way to grow your channel but you also need to give them a reason to subscribe. The obvious way is to just produce amazing videos that people can't resist...ok, sometimes a little easier said than done.

More powerful still is to make your channel a community. Make your channel a community where people can engage each other and share their opinions and you'll build more than a channel, you'll be building a movement!

A lot of the brand building ideas we talked about previously will come into play here. By connecting with those shared beliefs and through an iconic leader, you'll find people that will feel a special connection with your channel. Responding to comments and using the community tab, will cement that relationship.

You'll still need to ask people to subscribe but building this sense of community will make joining your channel a no-brainer for many. It may take a couple of videos before they actually click the button but talk up the inclusion and how great the community is and they'll click the button just to not be left out.

In fact, build a community around the channel and it will go a lot farther than just growing subscribers. You'll get cheerleaders that will share your videos with their friends. You'll have a constant base of comments on new videos and a rabid followership that will defend you against any trolls that dare speak ill of the channel.

Leveraging Social Media to Grow YouTube Subscribers

We highlighted a social media strategy for YouTube last week and getting subscribers is where that really starts paying off.

Platforms like Facebook and Twitter may have created the social media revolution but people are still looking for that face-to-face connection. They still want to feel included in a community and have true friends that are more than just a 'Like'.

That means sharing your videos on other social platforms isn't just about getting views but about bringing people over from those sites to join your YouTube community.

- Post community conversations regularly on Facebook and other platforms, something like a, "This is what we're talking about on YouTube."

- Talk up the growth of your YouTube channel community, posting images of subscriber milestones. I guarantee, anyone that sees 50,000 people have joined your channel is going to wonder if it might be right for them.

- Promote YouTube-only events and videos that won't be shared anywhere else.

Growing subscribers on YouTube doesn't have to be as complicated as most creators make it. You've given them a reason to subscribe through quality videos and a professional-looking channel. Most creators just need that last little nudge to send their subscriber growth into overdrive. For that, you've only got to ask and make it about the community.

Action Steps:

- Go back through your video structure template to make sure you include several opportunities to ask viewers to subscribe.

- Review and update your blog, and older blog posts if you have them, to include a call-to-action to subscribe to your channel.

- Join two or three Facebook groups related to your channel

niche and start becoming a valuable member. Answer and ask questions, respond to comments and become a member of the community.

WHY EVERY YOUTUBE CHANNEL NEEDS TO BE LIVE STREAMING

Live streaming on YouTube is becoming a must for any channel that wants to grow

Live streaming videos on YouTube can be a scary idea for many creators, even more so than the initial idea to start a channel. Recorded videos at least give you a chance to edit out the gaffes and other mistakes. Even someone new to being on film can look like an expert with good editing.

With live streaming, it's just you in all your flaws.

There are two big reasons why every YouTube creator needs to put live streams on their weekly schedule though. Live streaming will not only help develop your channel faster but it's that very personal nature that will help you build your community.

Let's take a look at both those reasons and then how to make live streaming as effortless as possible.

Why is Live streaming Important

YouTube first allowed live streaming in 2011, nearly six years after the first videos on the platform. For many years, going live with your audience was a novel but unnecessary option to growing a channel.

That's not the case anymore.

With the competition from millions of channels and new ones starting every day, live streaming is becoming a necessity on a couple of levels.

First is that live streaming helps you increase the frequency of your content. I saw a spike in traffic and subscribers each time I increased to an additional video per week, from one to two and then to three videos.

That increase might not be possible for many creators trying to juggle a full-time job as well as YouTube ambitions. If each scripted video takes you four hours to produce, publishing three a week would mean 12 hours on videos alone and wouldn't include all the social sharing and community building around a growing channel.

You can produce a 30-minute live stream in less than an hour including planning and social media sharing. That means publishing an extra day, more watch-time for your channel and faster growth.

More important though is that live streaming helps build a community like scripted videos never could. That downside to live stream, the full effect of all your gaffes and un-edited personality, is what makes the strategy so effective at pulling people into your tribe.

Live streams are up-close and personal. They build that relationship with your community and create a loyal band that will watch and promote your brand. Live streams give you a chance to reach your community on a personal level, answering questions and giving shout-outs to your fans.

As personal as a scripted video might seem, live streams take that relationship-building to the next level and simply cannot be overlooked.

How to Live stream on YouTube

The first time you go to live stream, you'll need to set up your equipment and connect a live streaming software.

You can live stream directly from the YouTube platform but I recommend using a streaming platform for a couple of reasons. Streaming from a platform like OBS will make your video look more professional through the use of graphics and screen transitions. These can dramatically increase your retention rate on videos because it's not just you sitting in front of the camera for an hour.

Let's look at how to set up your live stream first and then the planning around a specific video.

Setting up Your Live stream Platform

Download Open Broadcaster Software (OBS), free to download and use

Get your YouTube stream key and put in OBS (don't share with anyone ever)

Next go to your OBS dashboard and click 'Settings' in the lower-right menu. Here you'll see the 'Stream' menu in the left-menu and can enter your credentials.

- Choose YouTube/YouTube Gaming for your service
- Chose Primary YouTube ingest server
- Paste your stream key into the box and click Apply

Now you're able to stream from OBS directly onto your YouTube channel but you want to set some of the other controls on the platform.

First, you'll set your output resolution and bitrate on OBS. This will control how your video looks while streaming. A higher the resolution, frame rate and bit rate will mean higher needs for bandwidth and computer processing, maybe more than is available. Gamers will obviously need much higher rates here but most YouTube channels can get by with less.

- Click on 'Settings' and then 'Output' in the OBS menu
- Set your video bitrate at 1500 and the audio bitrate at 160
- Click on 'Video' in the menu and set your FPS value to 30 with a resolution of 1920x1080

An important setting is your audio input. The default input will be your computer and you need to change this if you're going to use another audio device like a microphone. Speaking from personal experience, make a habit of checking that your audio device is being used before starting your live stream. You don't want to get ten minutes into a stream and realize nobody could hear what you were saying.

To check your audio settings, just click 'Settings' then 'Audio' in the menu and find your preferred device in the input dropdown bar. When selected, you should see the colored Mic/Aux bar light up when you talk into the microphone.

OBS is really versatile software for live streaming. You can set up different scenes including screenshare and webcam capture. You can create scenes with different graphics like a scrolling banner prompting people to subscribe, live sub counts and community shout-outs. Take a little time to get to know the features and it'll make even the beginner live streamer look like a professional.

Getting Ready to Live stream

When it comes to actually streaming and what you'll talk about, don't overthink it. Remember, part of the benefit to live streaming is that it doesn't take as much time as scripted videos.

Take ten minutes to quickly outline what you want to talk about and maybe a layout for your stream. For example, I usually start by welcoming everyone and then get into some community shout-outs. I'll share a couple of comments I received over the week and maybe give a shout-out to another channel or two.

Then I'll outline a couple of broad topics I want to discuss, maybe reviewing the last week's videos or previewing the topics from the coming week. Finally I'll make time for community questions.

Outlining all this should take less than 20 minutes. That includes taking a screenshot of images you want to use, maybe from comments or other graphics.

The idea of sharing comments and community shout-outs is a great tool to build community. Even if someone doesn't hear their name or have their comment highlighted, you're still showing that you appreciate every individual person.

Don't worry too much about following the chat during the live stream. Larger channels may want to ask an assistant to moderate comments but smaller channels can go without. You can outsource the role or partner with another channel to moderate each other's streams. For most channels, you can just ask people to resubmit questions during the Q&A if you didn't see them earlier.

You'll want to create a thumbnail and meta-data for each live stream just like you would a regular video. In my experience, live streams don't get the views or have the long lifespan relative to regular videos but you'll still get post-stream views and will want to provide YouTube with that meta-data information. Do all this before the live stream and put it in your channel live page.

One last note for live streaming, relax and enjoy the chance to be closer to your community. It's live and people understand that means mistakes and bloopers. That's part of the appeal. The more human you are, the closer your community will feel with the channel.

Live streaming is no longer an optional feature for growing a YouTube channel. Not only will it help increase the frequency of your posting and grow channel watch-time, you'll develop a closer connection with your community. It's an invaluable part of the channel experience and one you can't neglect.

Action Steps:
- Download OBS Studio or another live streaming software.
- Set up OBS and connect it to your YouTube channel with the stream name. Create a couple of scenes you can use during a live stream.
- Do a test live stream, asking a few friends to attend, to see how the process works. Practice switching scenes in your live stream software and switching between graphics.

BUILDING A TEAM AND SCALING YOUR YOUTUBE CHANNEL

Growing a YouTube channel and your online business means outsourcing and letting go

Building a team around your online business, whether it be a YouTube channel or otherwise, is one of the most difficult decisions you'll face. Most of us start off as one-person working on a hobby project with no idea how a business in run.

Actually turning your YouTube channel into a scalable business is something completely foreign and maybe a little scary. It requires time, money and leads to more uncertainty than most of us want with our growing monthly income.

If you do want to reach your channel's potential though, there will come a time you need to start outsourcing the work. I haven't talked to a single creator with more than 200,000 subscribers that hasn't outsourced or developed a team around some aspect of the business.

YouTube Tasks that can be Outsourced

A note before we talk about which tasks can be outsourced. I'm using 'outsourced' and 'team' almost interchangeably here. The word 'team' implies someone that's a regular member and maybe has more buy-in than a freelancer to whom you outsource work occasionally.

I think of it as a progression though. You might start by outsourcing a task to a few freelancers before deciding to work with just one regularly. Over time, that person will become a trusted member of a more cohesive team even if you never see them in-person.

Editing is usually one of the first tasks YouTube creators decide to outsource. Editing can be tedious and involves skills a creator hasn't developed. It's also one of those tasks that can be handled without a full command of the English language, making it easily outsourced to lower-cost regions of freelancers.

When you're looking for video editors, make sure you ask for video references to see examples of their work. Scripting out your videos will make it easier because you can add production notes for where you want graphics and other assets to be placed.

Thumbnails are another task creators choose to outsource as their channel grows. Best practices say to keep your thumbnails consistent with structure and branding so it's relatively easy to reproduce images for new videos. Some freelancers will still require you to provide images and text copy for each thumbnail but the rest of the outsourcing process is straight-forward.

Promotion through social media, ads and collabs with other creators is a big step to outsource. It can also be one of the more expensive roles to hire but also worth it if you find someone with skills across social media and outreach.

Hiring promotion for your YouTube channel can actually be three different roles; social media, ads and collabs. They're all related so I've included them within an overall promotion role but you might start trying to find three separate freelancers specializing in their specific role.

- Social Media Strategy means not only sharing your videos across your social accounts but engaging in groups to promote the channel as well.

- Advertising includes building a measurable ad campaign for different platforms from YouTube to Google and social platforms. This doesn't mean you throw money at ads because you feel obligated to have an ad strategy but comes only after carefully considering the costs and return.

- YouTube Collabs are a great way to reach other audiences on the platform but can be difficult to set up. Finding someone with experience connecting people is worth the effort.

Here is where laying out responsibilities and trusting in the hiring process will be critical. We'll talk about this more in the next section but we're not talking about a quick or technical task like involved in thumbnail creation or editing. Promotion is a creative task and more than one way to do it. Even if you don't immediately agree with the strategy used by your new freelancer, give them time to grow into the role.

Comment moderation is another task easily outsourced though most channels use a process to answer different levels of comments. Typically an assistant will answer the easiest and most basic comments, those simply thanking you for your channel. The assistant will also delete spam comments and then mark remaining ones for the creator to answer.

Scripting and other parts of your content generation are usually the last to be outsourced. This is the value you bring to the table and it's usually quite expensive to find similar skills that can script videos in your natural voice.

Still, there are parts of your content that can be outsourced or at least can be worked on within the team. Assistants can help with idea generation, doing research on popular keywords on other channels and then researching ideas to be included in the video. Your entire team can all contribute ideas and direction for content strategy. You can pass the drafted script on to your members of the team for review and input on ways to engage and interest viewers.

How to Work with a Team

It's one thing to know what you want to outsource, it's something entirely different to be able to find people and work with a team effectively.

I'll warn you that putting an effective team together will be a frustrating and long-term project. You'll have to put up with people that don't perform and will have to rehire when valued members leave.

It's all part of running a business.

Put in the effort to be a manager rather than just a one-person operation and you will grow your business. Know that every other manager and business owner goes through the same frustrations. Your will be rewarded with higher income and a business that can function without you at the wheel 24/7.

We'll talk about setting up and managing your team next but understand there is another route you can take to this.

The alternative is hiring a business manager to handle everything you don't want to do. This is, of course, the more expensive option but can also free up your time to create content and do what you do best. You'll need someone that understands your business and is a good manager as well. You'll still need to be patient, letting them grow into the role and understand exactly what you want, but it's easier than managing the entire team yourself.

Whether you go with a business manager or not, the first step in working with a team is to set responsibilities, a process and goals for each role you want to fill.

- Write out exactly everything the person will do, assuming they come to the role with no prior knowledge. One great idea I've used is to create a video tutorial for each task.

- These different tasks will help you understand the responsibilities you want the role to bear and lay out goals for the hire to achieve.

- Of course, you and the hire want to evolve in the role over time. The best team member will be one that does their job and creates other tasks within the role that will drive growth.

This formalization of the role needs to be as detailed as possible before you begin looking for someone. It's going to make it crystal clear what you expect and what the freelancer needs to do.

Finding and selecting the right people is the easy...er, hard part. There are innumerable freelancer sites, some specific to a task while others are broader. I use Upwork but have also found people on Fiverr, Freelancer.com and through connections.

- Browse other job requests similar to yours so you have an idea of how much to offer

- Decide on all the special skill sets you want including English proficiency

- Detail your job description as much as possible and use any filters to prohibit people from applying if they do not meet requirements. Require some type of cover letter, their answer will help show you whether they actually read the description or are just replying with a template answer. Also require at least three references and contacts to prior work similar to your job.

Understand that for every 30 applicants to a job, you might only get a few worth interviewing and then maybe only one actually qualified for the job. Whatever you do, do not skip over parts in the hiring process. Time spent interviewing people and checking references is well spent compared to hiring the wrong person and then having to repeat the entire process in a month.

One method I've found that works well is to narrow your list of potential hires to a few well-qualified people, then have them all test on a small project. You'll still have to pay for them to perform the project but it will give you a better idea of how well they actually fit the role under a real assignment.

One important decision you'll need to make, at least starting out, will be the level of experience you want new hires to possess. You can hire someone able to do the job perfectly from day one but will generally have to pay more. You can hire someone with less developed skills but will spend more time training them for the role.

The most difficult part of the entire team-building process is after you hire someone for a role. Now comes the stage of training and development, a stage that will probably take at least three months.

This is where your new hire will need to work hard to learn the role but you'll also be tasked with being patient as they grow into it. Even someone with years of experience cannot be expected to know exactly how you want things done from day one.

Even more difficult will be accepting that your way may not be the best way. Keep an open mind to your new hire's ideas and be ready to accept change if it could help grow the business. It can be difficult to let go and let someone else take responsibility but this kind of proactive employee is the best kind to find.

You don't wake up one day and think to yourself, "I need a team for my YouTube channel." It's a slow realization that your time is better spent doing some tasks and not others. You'll start off by outsourcing one or two roles. Learn from the experience, being a better manager and slowly growing your team. One day you might wake up and think to yourself, "I really have a great team for my YouTube channel."

Action Steps:
- List out every step in your weekly YouTube process including

everything that goes into creating videos, managing your channel and promoting off-YouTube.

- Rank the list on tasks you most and least enjoy doing. Then rank it on tasks in which you feel like your strengths shine and tasks you don't do especially well. The tasks you least enjoy doing or those you feel like an expert could do much better are good potentials for outsourcing or hiring.

- Ask for recommendations for outsourcers in Facebook groups for YouTube creators.

- Review projects on Upwork to see how much similar jobs are paying and the detail behind job postings.

Get the Video Course and Get Started!

You've got everything you need in this book to grow a channel and make money...but sometimes that just isn't enough.

Time and again, I've seen would-be YouTube creators get started but something always seems to side-track them before they reach that level of success with their channel. Whether it's staying on schedule, finding the right help or just staying motivated, there is a minefield of obstacles that keeps them from realizing their dream.

That's why I wanted to offer the companion video course to the book! Through the videos, worksheets and especially the email series, you'll stay on track to start and grow your channel fast.

Think about it. If this video course helps you reach the point of making a few thousand on ads, sponsorships and affiliates just one money earlier than you would have otherwise...it will have paid for itself many times over.

Here's everything you'll get in the video course,

- Videos
- Worksheets for each chapter
- 8-week email series to keep you on schedule
- Lifetime access to the course, Q&A, resources and updates to always be on top of how to grow your channel
- Bonus channel review!

It's a great deal but only if you take advantage of it. Invest in your channel, stay on track and grow your channel and I guarantee you will be rewarded for it.

Watch this Free Preview Video and Get a Special 35% Discount

Or go to https://myworkfromhomemoney.com/YTCommunity

YOUTUBE RESOURCES TO PRODUCE AND MAKE MONEY WITH YOUR VIDEOS

It is surprisingly easy to make videos for YouTube but making professional-looking videos and ones that rank is something else entirely. You could shoot everything on your phone, upload to the platform and be done with it...or you can create an online asset to make a lot of money.

Below are the resources I use to run my YouTube business, from tools for researching the platform to making money and getting help. Most offer basic features for free and premium levels though you don't always need the premium levels to get as much out of the resources.

Resources for YouTube Research

TubeBuddy is the most popular YouTube software though VidIQ has some great features. I started with TubeBuddy and never really saw a need to change. All the features you need to do keyword research, monitor video rankings and check the SEO health of your channel. TubeBuddy is free to connect to your YouTube account and use the basic features.

VidIQ also has some solid features including its view velocity measures. I love the channel on YouTube and it's a great resource for tips. When I was starting my channel, the VidIQ website wasn't well developed so did not give me the confidence to use the software. I'd recommend trying it out to see how it differs from TubeBuddy though. Also free to download and use the basic features.

Resources for Video Editing

Camtasia is the video editing software I use though it is a bit expensive at $400 for a license. It's a one-time fee so not bad if you consider you'll use it on hundreds of videos. Solid features to make editing easy and make your videos look professional.

ScreenFlow is a free screen capture and video editing software that a lot of YouTube beginners choose to keep costs low. Doesn't have the features of Camtasia or Premiere Pro but solid no-cost option.

Resources for Making Money on YouTube

Affiliate Networks – This isn't a specific resource but a group you'll want to check out. Open an account on networks like CJ Affiliate, ShareASale and Rakuten Linkshare as soon as you start your YouTube channel. It might take a while to start seeing enough video views to translate into any real sales but affiliate marketing can be a big chunk of your income.

Teachable is a course hosting platform that allows you to collect payments, deliver your course and offer special price promotions. It's an all-in-one course platform and if you're already creating video content, why not reformat some of it into a paid course?

EverWebinar is a webinar hosting platform that allows you to record a live webinar and then make the replay look live. I use a recorded webinar as part of the sales funnel for all my courses and it makes the process completely passive. Click here for a special promotion, try it for 60 days for just $1

ConvertKit – I used three other email marketing tools and none of them had the features I needed, until ConvertKit. The site makes it easy to get email subscribers from your channel, send out automated email sequences and keep them in your funnel. Easily the best marketing tool for the money.

Bluehost – It always surprises me how many YouTube creators don't leverage the power of a blog. It's easy to transcribe and embed your videos as blog posts and it's a great way to create another online asset off YouTube.

I make thousands on my blogs each month and they provide easy [FREE] marketing for the channel. Launching a blog means you'll need to register a domain and get webhosting, both available through Bluehost.

Canva is a free design platform for creating thumbnails and social media graphics. The site has a premium membership level and sells some a la carte graphics for your images but you can get everything done for free.

While it's written for bloggers about making money in Make Money Blogging: 9 Proven Strategies to Make Money Online. The book goes step-by-step in setting up every income source I use on the blogs and YouTube channel to make six-figures a year. Get your copy on Kindle, Paperback or Audiobook.

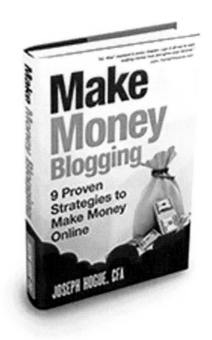

Finding Freelancers and Help with Your YT Channel

Upwork – is where I go to find most freelancers, especially if I already have a detailed idea of how I want the project to develop. The freelancer marketplace has its share of bad servicers but spend the time to interview and test for the right one and you'll build your team in no time.

Fiverr – I generally use Fiverr when I need help developing an idea. Since the projects are cheaper than hiring a freelancer on Upwork, I can buy a few 'gigs' to get ideas and test out different designs before going all-in on one. Works great for getting cover ideas and other design elements.

Thank You for Taking Me on Your Journey

Just one last note to say, Thank You, for starting your journey with me. I'm excited about what lies ahead and I know it's going to change your life.

There is no other income source I've enjoyed more than YouTube and no other has created the same level of passive income. The internet revolution has given us all the power to reach millions of people, transform lives and create the financial freedom we deserve.

Whether you're creating videos to become financially independent, help or entertain others, you'll be able to do it all with YouTube

I want to continue to be a part of your journey. Know that I'm always available to answer questions or just be a source for motivation when you need it. Reach out by email or through comments on the videos at Let's Talk Money on YouTube.

To your success,

Joseph Hogue

Joseph Hogue, CFA